William Wallace Martin

Reconstructive Criticism

A Theory to Reconcile the Difficulties of Higher Criticism

William Wallace Martin

Reconstructive Criticism
A Theory to Reconcile the Difficulties of Higher Criticism

ISBN/EAN: 9783337159290

Printed in Europe, USA, Canada, Australia, Japan

Cover: Foto ©Thomas Meinert / pixelio.de

More available books at **www.hansebooks.com**

Reconstructive Criticism.

A. THEORY TO RECONCILE THE DIFFICULTIES OF HIGHER CRITICISM.

BY

WILLIAM W. MARTIN,

FORMERLY PROFESSOR OF SEMITIC LANGUAGES IN
VANDERBILT UNIVERSITY.

CINCINNATI:

PRESS OF CURTS & JENNINGS.

I.

THE FAILURE OF THE MEDIATING SCHOOL.

OUR survey will be confined to the narrative portions of the
Old Testament. The prophetic and poetic portions will
not be considered. Higher Criticism rejects a Pentateuch and
accepts a Hexateuch. This result simply means, that the traditional view of the authorship of the first five books of the Bible
is abandoned. Hence, according to Higher Criticism, Moses·did
not write the Pentateuch. The denial of the authorship of these
books has in it no especial danger, so that there must needs spring
up, in consequence, a Mediating School. But the star scholars of
Higher Criticism deny with their proofs, not only the Mosaic
authorship of the Pentateuch, but also the credibility of these
books. Kuenen says, in regard to the description of the exodus
from Egypt, the wandering in the desert, the conquest and
partition of Canaan, that "their representations, to put it in a
word, are utterly unhistorical, and therefore can not have been
committed to writing until centuries after Moses and Joshua."

Our faith in Scripture as the word of God requires the credibility of what we read. There may be need of rearrangement,
confusion may have been worked into the books by the hand of
man; but the facts, for instance, of Moses' life, must be as credible as the facts which are recorded of the life of Christ. The
Mediating School attempts to demonstrate that Christians must
accept the data of destructive critics, and by a peculiar kind of
mental wriggling still hold to the credibility of the record.
Professor H. G. Mitchell, of Boston Theological School, is a
mediating critic. And he, in his *résumé* of the results of Higher
Criticism, says "that the Pentateuch is mainly composed of four
documents. Of these, the oldest are the Jahvistic, written in
Judah, and the Elohistic, written in Ephraim not long before or
after 800 B. C.; but which of them antedates the other is not yet
decided. These two became one about 600 B. C. And Deuteronomy, which had appeared in 621 B. C., but may have been

3

written in the reign of Manasseh, was then, or soon after that
time, incorporated into the same work.   The Priestly Document,
according to certain scholars, existed in some form before Deuteronomy was written; while others maintain that it was the
product of the Captivity; but most agree that it did not become
a part of the Pentateuch until a comparatively short time before
or after 444 B. C., the date of its promulgation in Ezra.   It should
be added that, as Deuteronomy was based on one or both of the
works that preceded it, the other documents are found to contain
materials much older than either of them; *so that there are
scholars who, while they accept the above statement, still feel
warranted in holding that the Pentateuch is, in a real sense,
Mosaic.*"

Professor Kuenen argues that the representations in the Pentateuch are utterly unhistorical, and therefore can not have been
committed to writing until centuries after Moses and Joshua.
Professor Mitchell argues that the two earliest documents were
written centuries after Moses; Deuteronomy is based on one or
both of these; and therefore is, *that there are scholars who feel
warranted in holding* "*that the Pentateuch is, in a real sense,
Mosaic.*"   The reader of his words naturally asks: How far are
the two earlier documents Mosaic? also, to what extent would a
document based upon them, two centuries later, be Mosaic? A
" Mosaic Pentateuch," resting on such a basis, would be a Pentateuch hardly flavored with Moses.   Professor Driver does some
splendid maneuvering with words in his effort to establish the
" value and authority of Deuteronomy as a part of the Old Testament canon, while denying to the book a Mosaic origin."   He
says also that, " in the first place, though it may appear paradox-
ical to say so, Deuteronomy does not claim to be written by
Moses."   Well, admit all this, nevertheless Deuteronomy requires
that we have, in the speeches attributed therein to Moses, his
words as truly as we have the words of Christ in the speeches of
Christ which John records.

There are certain facts connected with the Pentateuch which
Higher Criticism has clearly, definitively, and irrevocably established.   These may be briefly set forth as follows:

(1) There are duplicate narratives in these books of the same event, and these narratives are written from a standpoint entirely different.

(2) There are in some narratives two narratives, at least, combined, so that confusion is apparent and differences appear, such as make it unreasonable to affirm that the narrative was written in its present form by a single writer.

(3) There are misplacements of events, and so remarkable that Professor Mitchell may write truly the following: " The story that Abimelech, attracted by the beauty of Sarah, took her from her supposed brother to his harem, is not in itself improbable. The difficulty in believing it arises from the fact that it is so placed as to make it appear, from data taken from other sources, that she was nearly ninety years of age." Yet a misplacement of a fact does not invalidate the fact ; and a critic's aim should be to replace things so that incongruities are removed, thus leaving the fact and all connected with it probable. There are also different religious customs and various religious teachings in the Pentateuch, which, without doubt, belong to times later by centuries than the times which belong to the Pentateuch.

These all are facts, which may be verified by any one. The simple vital question is, How can we explain the production of books having these unusual and undeniable peculiarities? Higher Criticism proffers us this answer. It says: " There are sections homogeneous in style and character with Gen. i, 1—ii, 4, which recur at intervals, not in Genesis only, but in the following books to Joshua inclusive. Read consecutively, they are found to contain a nearly complete whole, and constitute the framework of our present Hexateuch." Higher Critics designate this narrative by the letter " P." There remains, after the separation of " P," "narratives which are not homogeneous in structure. Indeed, they exhibit marks of composition; and in some portions the welding is so closely made that the marks of demarkation between them frequently can not be fixed with certainty." Higher Criticism concludes that this portion, which remains after the separation of ' " P," is the combination of two narratives, originally independent, though covering largely the same ground, which have been united by a subsequent editor, who himself made some inconsiderable additions. One of these narratives is indicated by the letter "E," and the other by the letter "J." The combined narrative is called "JE." Deuteronomy stands alone, and is referred to under the letter "D." Such is the answer which Higher Criticism gives us to explain the diverse phenomena which meet us in the Hexateuch, and, of course, in the Pentateuch. The scholars who have made the greatest name by the so-called separation of the "component elements of the Hexateuch" deny, in view of this mode of composition, the entire trustworthiness of the record as history. The Mediating School, accepting the same theory of the composition of these books, seek to show how Christians may receive the results of Higher Criticism, and still accept the records "in a real sense as Mosaic," or in a real sense as historically credible. There can be but one judgment upon this work of the Mediating School. Their work is failure. One who is a prominent minister, and with recognized high scholarship, utters these words: "The traditional view of the origin of the present Pentateuch may require modification; but the present Mediating School can not be said to have defended the credibility of the Old Testament and its claims to being the record of a Divine revelation against the assaults of the destructive critics."

The Christian Church is not prepared to abandon faith in the credibility of the Old Testament. It will believe in the facts of the Old Testament, even if it admits, as it must, that these facts have been crowded into a conglomerate mass somehow and sometime. It will await undisturbed a disentanglement of these facts, which will not destroy their credibility. It will meanwhile learn of God from these facts, just as a geologist learns truth from fragments of stone which the storms and other forces have carried away from the place where they were formed. The present series of papers will set forth a theory which, while it recognizes the confusion pointed out by Higher Criticism, will account for it, and at the same time indicate the method of removing the difficulties arising therefrom. It may be said that the theory is based on what may be called Reconstructive Criticism.

This theory, placed in briefest paragraph, is: There were

originally two histories of Israel. The sources of the facts contained in them need not at present be considered any more than we need to know the sources of the facts of Thucydides and Herodotus. Hence this theory is not incumbered with letters to represent documents, and these same letters written with "primes and seconds," to indicate redactors. A large portion of these two histories of Israel have remained almost intact, and may be found in the Books of the Chronicles and portions, parallel to them, in 2 Samuel and in the Books of the Kings. We have, in the present form of the Pentateuch, in Joshua, Judges, and in 1 Samuel, a unification of these two histories, made by authorities who felt justified to unite the two works in these parts. The duplicate narratives, the contrary statements in the same narrative, the confusions, are explained by misplacements to accomplish this unification. The illustrations of Reconstructive Criticism, which we will give, can not of course go in detail over this vast field. Yet enough will be presented to impress the reader with the conviction that the theory rests upon careful investigation and approved scholarship. The writer has provisionally separated the whole of these two histories, and he has critically separated them in the Pentateuch. This personal statement may be pardoned, since it is necessary to indicate how far this theory rests on already accomplished investigations. The following pages will set forth investigations, illustrating how two narratives may be combined and make a third narrative consistent in its parts; how Reconstructive Criticism separates into two narratives the meeting of Jacob and Rachel at the well; and how the Song of Moses is recorded in each history ; then will follow the accounts of Creation, of the Generations of Adam, and of the Flood.

The argumentative force of these articles will be along this line. If, where inconsistencies are apparent, these are removed, and from one composite narrative or poem two are shown to be present, which are full of detail and present important teachings from a different standpoint, obtained from one event, it lays a fair presumption that this method of research may remove the principal difficulties which are alleged against the Pentateuch.

Again, if it may be proved that we have two histories of Israel, giving as full details of the events in this people's national life as we have of the details of the life of Christ in the Gospels of Matthew and Luke, then one history confirms the credibility of the other; and we have the historical portions of the Old Testament ratified by two separate and distinct accounts. This theory, then, will give us in the Pentateuch; not some words used in the Mosaic sense, but the words of Moses as truly as we have the words of Christ in the Gospels.

II.

THE UNIFICATION OF TWO NARRATIVES ILLUSTRATED.

THE occurrence which has wrought inconsistencies and confusion in the first books of Scripture, and which Higher Criticism has minutely specified, especially in the Hexateuch, was, according to the theory which we advance, a unification of two histories of Israel. It is purposed in this article to combine two New Testament narratives, making one which is complete and homogeneous. This unification will involve no change of the forms which are given in the Greek, and will embody all the words in the two narratives as they appear in the two Gospels.

What is common to both narratives will appear, of course, only once in the composite narrative. It should be said, in passing, that the unification in the Pentateuch is everywhere as conscientiously made as possible. There is nothing omitted, but everything which is found in the original histories is retained in the unified narrative. There is no change in the forms of the words as these forms appear in the Hebrew. There are no interpolations, except that those who made this unification added, perhaps, the conjunction for "and," or the phrases, "He said," "They said," or the equivalents of these. We have simply two histories united together without alteration or addition, making sometimes narratives without inconsistencies, except repetition of the same events in different words, or with inconsistencies which are irreconcilable. The unification of these two histories of Israel, without alteration of them, bespeaks, with remarkable emphasis, the sacredness of these records to those who made them, for some sufficient reason, into one narrative.

The New Testament narratives which we take, will be those written by Matthew and Luke, and describing the healing of the centurion's servant.

9

Matthew records the incident in these words:

> And when Jesus was entered into Capernaum, there came unto him a centurion, beseeching him saying, Lord, my servant lieth at home sick of the palsy, grievously tormented. And Jesus saith unto him, I will come and heal him. The centurion answered and said, Lord, I am not worthy that thou shouldst come under my roof; but speak the word only, and my servant shall be healed. For I am a man under authority, having soldiers under me: and I say to this man, Go, and he goeth; and to another, Come, and he cometh; and to my servant, Do this, and he doeth. When Jesus heard, he marveled, and said to them that followed, Verily I say unto you, I have not found so great faith, no, not in Israel. And I say unto you, That many shall come from the east and west, and shall sit down with Abraham, and Isaac, and Jacob, in the kingdom of heaven; but the children of the kingdom shall be cast out into outer darkness: there shall be weeping and gnashing of teeth. And Jesus said unto the centurion, Go thy way; and as thou hast believed, so be it done unto thee. And his servant was healed in the selfsame hour. (Matt. viii, 5–13.)

Luke records this event in these words:

> Now, when he had ended all his sayings in the audience of the people, he entered into Capernaum. And a certain centurion's servant, who was dear unto him, was sick and ready to die. And when he heard of Jesus, he sent unto him the elders of the Jews, beseeching him that he would come and heal his servant. And when they came to Jesus, they besought him instantly, saying, That he was worthy for whom he should do this: for he loveth our nation, and he hath built us a synagogue. Then Jesus went with them. And when he was now not far from the house, the centurion sent friends to him, saying unto him, Lord, trouble not thyself; for I am not worthy that thou shouldst enter under my roof: wherefore, neither thought I myself worthy to come unto thee: but say in a word, and my servant shall be healed. For I also am a man set under authority, having under me soldiers, and I say unto one, Go, and he goeth; and to another, Come, and he cometh; and to my servant, Do this, and he doeth. When Jesus heard these things, he marveled at him, and turned him about, and said unto them that followed him, I say unto you, I have not found so great faith, no, not in Israel. And they that were sent, returning to the house, found the servant whole that had been sick. (Luke vii, 1–10.)

There are marked differences in these two narratives. We notice that Matthew gives us more of the words of Christ and less of the doings of men; while Luke reverses, giving us more of the deeds of men and fewer of the words of Christ. Matthew makes no mention of the two deputations sent to Christ. Luke records no words, such as, "And I say unto you, That many shall come from the east and the west," etc. In presenting the unification of these two narratives, what belongs to Matthew alone we shall place in ordinary type; what belongs to Luke alone, in italics; what is common to both, in small capitals. It will then be seen at a glance, the displacement required to unite them into a homogeneous and consistent narrative. The following is the composite narrative:

Luke 1-3 a.   *Now when he had ended all his sayings in the audience of the people, he entered into Capernaum. And a certain centurion's servant, who was dear unto him, was sick and ready to*

Matt. 5 a.   *die. And when he heard concerning Jesus,* he having entered

Luke 3 b-7. into Capernaum, *he sent unto him the elders of the Jews, beseeching him that he would come and heal his servant. And when they came to Jesus, they besought him instantly, saying, That he was worthy for whom he should do this: for he loveth our nation, and he hath built us a synagogue. Then Jesus went with them. And when he was now not far from the house, the centurion sent friends to him, saying unto him, Lord, trouble not thyself; for I am not worthy that thou shouldst enter under my roof: wherefore neither thought I myself worthy to come unto thee: but say the word, and my servant shall be healed*

Matt. 5 b-8. Then the centurion came unto him, beseeching him, saying, Lord, my servant lieth at home sick of the palsy, grievously tormented. And Jesus saith unto him, I will come and heal him. And the centurion answered and said, Lord, I am not worthy that thou shouldst come under my roof; but speak the

Luke 8. word only, and my servant shall be healed. FOR I ALSO AM A

Matt. 9-10 a. MAN *set* UNDER AUTHORITY, HAVING UNDER ME SOLDIERS: AND

Luke 8-9 a. I SAY UNTO ONE, GO, AND HE GOETH; AND TO ANOTHER, COME, AND HE COMETH; AND TO MY SERVANT, DO THIS, AND HE

Luke 9. DOETH. WHEN JESUS HEARD *these things,* HE MARVELED *at him,* AND *turning to the crowd that followed him,* HE SAID

Matt. 10. to them that followed him, Verily, I SAY UNTO YOU, I HAVE NOT

Luke 9. FOUND SO GREAT FAITH, NO, NOT IN ISRAEL. And I say unto

Matt. 11-13. you, That many shall come from the east and west, and shall sit down with Abraham, and Isaac, and Jacob, in the kingdom of heaven: but the children of the kingdom shall be cast out into outer darkness: there shall be weeping and gnashing of teeth. And Jesus said unto the centurion, Go thy way; and as thou hast believed, so be it done unto thee. And his servant was healed in that selfsame hour. *And they that were sent, returning, found the servant healed that had been sick.*

Luke 10.

At a glance, it will be seen how little of labor it required to construct this composite narrative. Yet if we had this narrative, and were undertaking to disentangle therefrom the narrative of Matthew and the narrative of Luke, any one can see what a difficult task would be placed before us. We would need to know the peculiar point of view which each writer held; the details which attracted each most powerfully; and many, many other particulars. The chief difficulties in the undertaking would arise through the almost perfect consistency of this composite narrative. Therefore, if our theory respecting the Pentateuch be true, the grave difficulties arising from the clashings of different portions of any narrative, such as Higher Criticism speaks of in order to prove the narratives utterly untrustworthy, become the most helpful aids in unraveling the two original histories.

Our next article will separate the two narratives, which are present in the description of Jacob and Rachel at the well, as this event is recorded in Genesis.

III.

RECONSTRUCTIVE CRITICISM.

THE TWO ACCOUNTS OF JACOB AND RACHEL AT THE WELL.

THESE two accounts are bound together in one narrative. The incongruities found here have not been sufficiently obtrusive to impress the popular mind as is the case in many other portions of the Pentateuch, because the love-at-first-sight, which fettered both Rachel and Jacob, has been for all readers the charming congruity in the narrative. The common inheritance of the Christian mind, from the words in this passage, is a picture in which a well is central, surrounded by reclining flocks with their shepherds, and a stranger standing among them, talking with the keepers of the sheep. As soon as a beautiful maiden approaches, leading her father's sheep to the well, this stranger breaks off conversation with the shepherds, and goes to the well, rolls away the great stone at the mouth of the well, and waters for the beautiful shepherdess the flock which she tends. Her rare beauty wins the stranger; his graceful courtesy and large strength win the maiden. This is the meeting of Jacob and Rachel at the well. Ancestry is a mighty factor in a race. Courtesy, strength, beauty, and passionate admiration of these traits in the individual, ought to be a birthright of Joseph and Benjamin; for they are the children of Jacob and Rachel. The splendid career of Joseph and the majesty of Ephraim and Manasseh, manifest to all that they did not sell their birthright for a mess of pottage or of pleasure.

The composite narrative, which is found in Gen. xxix, 1–13, contains conflicting statements. For instance, it is said, in the third verse, that the flocks were watered; while, in the eighth verse, it is clearly implied that the flocks had not been watered. Then there is a difficulty in the words of Jacob in the twelfth verse. The shepherds had told him that Rachel was the daughter of Laban. It was enough to justify his formal kissing of Rachel,

13

and his weeping afterward, when he said to her, "I am your
father's brother." His information from the shepherds would
lead him to say so much, and no more. Yet Jacob adds, "I am
Rebekah's son." We will now give the two narratives as they
appear when separated; then we will present the whole composite narrative as it is found in Genesis.

For convenience we will name one of these separated narratives "E," and the other "J." The italics in each narrative will
show what in it is common to both narratives. The numerals
on the margin refer to verses in this Scripture.

The narrative of "E :"

Verses 1, 2.   *Then Jacob went on his journey, and came to the land of
the people of the East. And he looked, and behold a well in the*
Verse 2.   *field;* and lo! there were three flocks of sheep lying by it; for
out of that well they watered the flocks: and a great stone
Verses 7-9.   was upon the mouth of the well. And he said, Lo! it is yet
high day, neither is it time that the cattle should be gathered together; water the flock, and go feed them. And they said: We
can not, until all the flocks be gathered together, and till they
roll the stone from the well's mouth; then we water the sheep.
And while he yet spake with them, Rachel came with her
Verse 10.   father's sheep; for she kept them. *Then Jacob went near, and*
rolled the stone from the well's mouth, and watered the flocks
Verse 12.   of Laban, his mother's brother. *And Jacob told Rachel* that he
was Rebekah's son: *and she ran and told her father. And it*
Verse 13.   *came to pass, when Laban heard the tidings of Jacob,* his sister's
son, *that he ran to meet him, and embraced him, and kissed
him,* and brought him to his house. *And he told Laban all
those things.*

The narrative of "J :"

Verses 1, 2.   *Then Jacob went on his journey, and came to the land of
the people of the East. And he looked, and behold a well in the*
Verses 3-6.   *field.* And thither were all the flocks gathered; and they rolled
away the stone from the well's mouth, and watered the sheep,
and put the stone on the well's mouth in his place. And Jacob
said unto them, My brethren, whence be ye? And they said unto
him, Of Haran are we. And he said unto them, Know ye Laban
the son of Nahor? And they said, We know him. And he said
unto them, Is he well? And they said, He is well: and, behold,
Verses 10-12.   Rachel, his daughter, cometh with his sheep. And it came to
pass, when Jacob saw Rachel, the daughter of Laban his mother's
brother, and the sheep of Laban his mother's brother, that

Verse 10.   *Jacob went near*, and kissed Rachel, and lifted up his voice and
Verse 12.   wept. *And Jacob told Rachel* that he was her father's brother:
Verses 12, 13. *and she ran and told her father.* *And it came to pass that,
            when Laban heard the tidings of Jacob, that he ran to meet
Verse 14.   him, and embraced him, and kissed him.* And Laban said to
            him, Surely thou art my bone and my flesh. And he abode
            with him the space of a month. *And he told Laban all those
            things.*

   The most cursory reading of these two narratives will show
that this episode at the well is pictured with entirely different
feeling. "E" is full of merriest humanity, while "J" is just as
proper as the staidest and most precise people would require.
The facts in each narrative are the same: Jacob meets Rachel at
the well; they become acquainted at the well; and at the well
Laban meets Jacob, and brings him hence to his house. The
narratives are also alike in that the well has a great stone upon
its mouth, and the keepers of the sheep wait until several are
come together, and then the stone is rolled away, the flocks
watered, and afterwards the stone is replaced. But all else varies.
In the narrative of "E" the keepers of the sheep are shepherdesses; but in "J" they are shepherds. Jacob, in "E," chides
the shepherdesses for loitering at the well, and they respectfully
give him reason for waiting there with their flocks. Also in
"E," Jacob, attracted by Rachel's beauty, gracefully goes, removes
the stone, and waters her flock. And in the conversation
which takes place, he tells her that he is Rebekah's son. Rachel,
hearing this, runs to her home and tells the news. "J" pursues
his narrative differently. We find in "J," Jacob conversing with
the shepherds at the well, calling them "My brethren;" and
learning from them that Laban is in good health; and that Rachel,
his daughter, approaches with her father's sheep. Thereupon
Jacob meets her, kisses her, weeps, and tells her that he is her
father's brother. The kiss, proffered as a sign of relationship,
was then, as now, an exceedingly proper public manifestation of
kinship ties. The narrative of "E" is otherwise, and has in it
the simple charms of love. A beautiful girl attracts by her
simple beauty the worthy admiration of a noble man. Native
courtesy toward the beauty impels this gentle man to render
helpful service. They discover in the pleasant speech of the

moment that they are related. Then she hurries from him to
tell her father. Rachel is charming in her modest coyness; for
she makes no show of gladness before Jacob, except that she
runs home to tell her father.

It remains for us to give the narrative as it appears composite
in Genesis, showing the narrative of "E" with common type,
the narrative of "J" with italics, and representing what is common to both narratives by small capitals. This will have the
advantage of showing to the eye the composition.

The composite narrative:

THEN JACOB WENT ON HIS JOURNEY, AND CAME TO THE
LAND OF THE PEOPLE OF THE EAST. AND HE LOOKED, AND
BEHOLD A WELL IN THE FIELD; and lo! there were three flocks
of sheep lying by it; for out of that well they watered the
flocks: and a great stone was upon the well's mouth. *And
thither were all the flocks gathered: and they rolled the stone
from the well's mouth, and watered the sheep, and put the stone
again upon the well's mouth in his place. And Jacob said unto
them, My brethren, whence be ye? And they said, Of Haran
are we. And he said unto them, Know ye Laban the son of
Nahor? And they said, We know him. And he said unto
them, Is he well? And they said, He is well: and, behold,
Rachel, his daughter, cometh with the sheep.* And he said, Lo! it
is yet high day; neither is it time that the cattle should be gathered together: water ye the sheep, and go and feed them. And
they said, We can not, until all the flocks be gathered together,
and till they roll the stone from the well's mouth: then we
water the sheep. And while he yet spake with them, Rachel
came with her father's sheep; for she kept them. *And it came
to pass, when Jacob saw Rachel, the daughter of Laban his
mother's brother, and the sheep of Laban his mother's brother,
that Jacob kissed Rachel, and lifted up his voice and wept.*
JACOB WENT NEAR, and rolled away the stone from the well's
mouth, and watered the flocks of Laban his mother's brother.
And Jacob kissed Rachel, and lifted up his voice and wept.
AND JACOB TOLD RACHEL *that he was her father's brother, and*
that he was Rebekah's son: AND SHE RAN AND TOLD HER
FATHER. AND IT CAME TO PASS, WHEN LABAN HEARD THE
TIDINGS OF JACOB his sister's son, THAT HE RAN TO MEET HIM,
AND EMBRACED HIM, AND KISSED HIM, and brought him to his
house; and he told Laban all those things. *And Laban said
to him, Surely thou art my bone and my flesh. And he abode
with him the space of a month.*

Higher Criticism finds basis for its analysis of Genesis into documents, such as "E," "J," "JE," which have suffered from redactors, which it also recognizes, in just such inconsistencies as appear in this narrative, which we have shown to be a composition of two narratives without any changes, and by employing only the right to rearrange the parts of the two narratives, and unifying these parts into a single piece. Professor Driver (and he in his analysis departs in no great measure from Kuenen and Wellhausen) refers the whole of this narrative, which we have studied, to "J." What a strange writing "J" must be, if this is a fair sample according to Higher Criticism! Yet, on the theory here presented, how easily difficulties vanish!

IV.

RECONSTRUCTIVE CRITICISM.

The Two Records of Moses' Song.

ONE service, surely, Higher Criticism has done—it has kicked up a great dust. Another more valuable service is, that it has faced Christians boldly, and declared that the Bible, which is the basis of their faith, abounds in strangest inconsistencies. The greatest service is, that Higher Criticism has been the leader in those investigations which are preparatory to that rearrangement of Scripture which will show the orderly development of the marvelous revelation to the Hebrews concerning Jehovah and his doings among men. Reconstructive Criticism must take the place of Higher Criticism; yet not its place, except as the edifice absorbs attention, although the great stairway leading to it be a marvel of patient and laborious masonry.

There can be no doubt but that the passage chosen for this article is difficult. For consider what scholars have said in regard to this song. They say it is an expansion by later times of a Mosaic theme. Hand after hand touched it up, until it has taken its present form. We claim that the song is a national religious poem, and of great antiquity; that there are two versions essentially alike, with differences no more striking than the differences present in narratives of the same event in Christ's life which may be found in the Gospels. Here, however, is not the place to explain the differences in its versions. We will give, first, the version which is found in " E " (using thus the same mode of designation as in our previous articles), and, where anything is common, we will place it in italics. The poetic lines are referred to their appropriate verses on the margin.

The Version of " E."

I.

Verse 1.
I will sing of the Lord,
For he has triumphed gloriously;
The horse and his rider

18

He hath thrown into the sea.
Verse 2.   He is my father's God,
Verse 3.   Jehovah is his name,
Verse 2.   And I will praise him.

II.

Verse 8.   With the blast of thy nostrils
The waters were piled up.
Verse 9.   *The enemy said:*
I will pursue and overtake,
I will divide the spoil.
Verse 10. Thou didst blow with thy breath,
The sea covered them;
They sank in the mighty waters as lead.

III.

Verse 15. Trembling taketh the mighty men of Moab;
All the inhabitants of Canaan melt away,
Terror and dread falleth upon them.
Verse 11. Who is like thee, O Lord, among the gods?
Who is like thee, glorious in holiness,
Fearful in praises, doing wonders?

IV.

Verse 13. Thou in thy mercy leadest
The people which thou hast redeemed.
Verse 16. When thy people pass over, O Lord,
Thou shalt plant them in the mountain of thy inheritance,
Verse 17. The place for thy dwelling, which thou hast made, O Lord.

THE VERSION OF "J."

I.

Verse 2.   The Lord is my strength and song,
And he is become my salvation.
Verse 4.   Pharaoh's chariot and his hosts
He hath cast into the sea,
And his chosen captains are sunk in the Red Sea.
The deeps have covered them;
They went down into the depths like a stone.
Verse 2.   This one, my God, is Jehovah,
Verses 3, 2. A man of war, and I will praise him.

II.

Verse 8   The floods stood upright as a heap,
           The deep was congealed in the heart of the sea.
Verse 9.   *The enemy said:*
           My desire shall be satisfied upon them;
           I 'll draw my sword, my hand shall destroy them.
Verse 12. Thou stretchedst forth thy right hand,
           The earth swallowed them.
Verse 16. By the might of thy right hand
           They are made silent as a stone.

III.

Verse 14. The peoples have heard, they tremble;
           Pangs seize the inhabitants of Philistia;
           The dukes of Edom are amazed.
Verse 6.   Thy right hand, O Lord, is glorious in power,
           Thy right hand, O Lord, dasheth down thy enemy;
Verse 7.   And in thy full majesty thou overthrowest revolters;
           Thou sendest forth thy wrath, it consumes them as stubble.

IV.

Verse 16. Until the people which thou hast purchased pass over,
Verse 13. Thou guidest them with strength;
Verse 17. Thou wilt bring them into thy holy habitation,
           Thy sanctuary, O Lord, which thy hands have established.
Verse 18. The Lord shall reign for ever and ever.

Before indicating by different types how these two poems were combined into one, certain likenesses in the two poems should be indicated. They have the same number of strophes, four in all. Each strophe has the same subject-matter essentially, but with striking differences of verbal expression. The two poems are characterized therefore by peculiar differences of style; yet only such as might appear in a translation, made by two persons from different standpoints of view and of education. One may readily test the essential likeness of these two poems by reading corresponding strophes together. We will now present the composite poem, representing " E " with the ordinary type; " J " with italics; and what is common between them, by small capitals.

THE POEMS IN COMPOSITION:

THEN SANG MOSES AND THE CHILDREN OF ISRAEL THIS SONG
     UNTO THE LORD, AND SPAKE, SAYING:

I will sing of the Lord,
For he hath triumphed gloriously.
The horse and his rider
He hath thrown into the sea.
The Lord is my strength and song,
And he is become my salvation.
This one, my God, and I will praise him,
My father's God and I will exalt him.
The Lord is a man of war.
Jehovah is his name.
Pharaoh's chariot and his hosts
He hath cast into the sea,
And his chosen captains are sunk into the Red Sea;
The deeps have covered them;
They went down into the depths like a stone.
Thy right hand, O Lord, is glorious in power;
Thy right hand, O Lord, dasheth down thy enemy,
And in thy full majesty thou overthrowest revolters;
Thou sendest forth thy wrath, it consumes them as stubble.
With the blast of thy nostrils
The waters were piled up;
The floods stood upright as a heap,
And the deeps were congealed in the heart of the sea.

THE ENEMY SAID:

I will pursue and overtake;
I will divide the spoil
My desire shall be satisfied upon them;
I'll draw my sword, my hand shall destroy them.
Thou didst blow with thy breath,
The sea covered them;
They sank in the mighty waters as lead.
Who is like unto thee, O Lord, among the gods?
Who is like unto thee, glorious in holiness,
Fearful in praises, doing wonders?

Thou stretchedst forth thy right hand,
The earth swallowed them.
Thou in thy mercy leadest
The people which thou hast redeemed;
Thou dost guide them in thy strength
Into thy holy habitation.

The peoples have heard, they tremble;
Pangs seize the inhabitants of Philistia,
The dukes of Edom are amazed.
Trembling taketh the mighty men of Moab;
All the inhabitants of Canaan melt away,
Terror and dread falleth upon them.
By the might of thy right hand
They were made as silent as a stone.
When thy people pass over, O Lord,
Until thy people which thou hast purchased pass over,
Thou wilt bring them . . .
Thou wilt plant them in the mountain of thine inheritance,
The place for thy dwelling which thou hast made, O Lord;
The sanctuary which thy hands have established.
The Lord shall reign for ever and ever.

All which was proposed in these articles has been done. The passages taken are passages where scholars have not even surmised the presence of a duplicate narrative. The resolution of this poem into its two component parts has been more difficult, of course, than the separation of the narative concerning Rachel and Jacob at the well. These investigations, therefore, are sufficient in extent, because of the peculiar difficulties involved in them, arising from the fact that they have heretofore been considered one production, but modified by the hands of redactors to win confidence in reconstructive criticism. God is not the author of confusion; neither do his servants, when revealing his ways among men, utter oracles which are a hodge-podge. The Phariseeism of the Jews may have wrought in the Old Testament confusion; but it was not by alteration—it was simply by misplacement. It is the task of Christian scholarship to reconstruct the oracles of God, and set them in the noble forms which they had when prophet and inspired poet first gave them to believing and unbelieving times. The undertaking is arduous; its charm most alluring; its reward, profound thankfulness that God has revealed his Word in harmonies vaster than those which the scientific mind finds everywhere prevalent in the physical world —vaster, even, than those harmonies in nature which the beautiful flowers and the shining stars have been first to disclose to the devout and studious mind.

V.

RECONSTRUCTIVE CRITICISM.

THE TWO RECORDS OF CREATION: THE GENERATIONS OF ADAM, AND THE FLOOD.

IN order to give ampler opportunity for the testing of the theory advanced and advocated by Reconstructive Criticism, we have arranged for this pamphlet our investigations as they were made in connection with the earlier chapters of Genesis. We express our heartiest regret that the Hebrew will be found abounding in many mistakes. These have occurred because of retracing on the part of the engraver. Those, however, who are unacquainted with the Hebrew will not be offended by these errors; while Hebrew scholars will gladly pardon them because of the help even a defective text will give. The labor required by these investigations will be immediately recognized by that large company of noble scholars who have given years of toil to the Hebrew records. It is not to be hoped that Reconstructive Criticism will win recognition without the severest testing. Scholarship will measure fairly its claims. The theory set forth in these pages must contend, not alone with the multitude, who have regarded the higher critics as "destroyers of the faith," but also with these higher critics themselves. Verily, the hosts arrayed against Reconstructive Criticism are legion. But truth in the end triumphs, and the present investigations were made in loving search after truth.

The method of setting forth the results of Reconstructive Criticism, as it has been applied to these earlier narratives of Genesis, is to place upon one page the Prophetic Narrative, and upon its opposite page the Priestly Narrative. There have been added foot-notes, not with any thought of giving complete discussion, but only to call attention to certain facts in the way of comparison, or for some other clearly apparent reason. Much will be desired on the part of scholars, which the limits set to these investigations have prevented us from giving; but enough is furnished to call forth, on the part of those who pursue these subjects of criticism, a considerate attention to the theory which Reconstructive Criticism propounds.

23

Reconstructive Criticism.

Illustrated by Genesis.

CREATION.

I, 1 In the beginning God created
2 the heaven and the earth. And
the earth was waste and void;
and darkness was upon the face
3 of the deep. And God said, Let
there be light: and there was light.
4 And God saw the light, that it was
good: and God divided the light
5 from the darkness. And God called
the light Day, and the darkness he
called Night. And there was evening and there was morning, one
6 day. And God said, Let there be
a firmament in the midst of the
waters, and let it divide the waters
from the waters. And it was so.
And God saw that it was good.
7 And God called the firmament
8 Heaven. And there was evening
and there was morning a second
9 day. And God said, Let the waters under the heaven be gathered
together to one place, and let the
10 dry land appear. And God called
the dry land Earth; and the gath-
ering together of the waters called
11 he Seas. And God said, Let the
earth put forth grass, herb yielding
seed, fruit tree bearing fruit after
its kind, wherein is the seed thereof,
12 upon the earth: and it was so. And
13 God saw that it was good. And there
was evening and there was morn-
14 ing, a third day. And God said,

בְּרֵאשִׁית בָּרָא אֱלֹהִים אֵת
הַשָּׁמַיִם וְאֵת הָאָרֶץ: וְהָאָרֶץ
הָיְתָה תֹהוּ וָבֹהוּ וְחֹשֶׁךְ עַל־
פְּנֵי תְהוֹם: וַיֹּאמֶר אֱלֹהִים יְהִי
אוֹר וַיְהִי־אוֹר: וַיַּרְא אֱלֹהִים
אֶת־הָאוֹר כִּי־טוֹב וַיַּבְדֵּל
אֱלֹהִים בֵּין הָאוֹר וּבֵין הַחֹשֶׁךְ:
וַיִּקְרָא אֱלֹהִים לָאוֹר יוֹם
וְלַחֹשֶׁךְ קָרָא לָיְלָה: וַיְהִי־עֶרֶב
וַיְהִי־בֹקֶר יוֹם אֶחָד: וַיֹּאמֶר
אֱלֹהִים יְהִי רָקִיעַ בְּתוֹךְ הַמַּיִם
וִיהִי מַבְדִּיל בֵּין מַיִם לָמָיִם:
וַיְהִי־כֵן: וַיַּרְא אֱלֹהִים כִּי־
טוֹב: וַיִּקְרָא אֱלֹהִים לָרָקִיעַ
שָׁמַיִם: וַיְהִי־עֶרֶב וַיְהִי־בֹקֶר
יוֹם שֵׁנִי: וַיֹּאמֶר אֱלֹהִים יִקָּווּ
הַמַּיִם מִתַּחַת הַשָּׁמַיִם אֶל־מָקוֹם
אֶחָד וְתֵרָאֶה הַיַּבָּשָׁה: וַיִּקְרָא
אֱלֹהִים לַיַּבָּשָׁה אֶרֶץ וּלְמִקְוֵה
הַמַּיִם קָרָא יַמִּים: וַיַּרְא אֱלֹהִים
אֱלֹהִים תַּדְשֵׁא הָאָרֶץ דֶּשֶׁא
עֵשֶׂב מַזְרִיעַ זֶרַע עֵץ פְּרִי
עֹשֶׂה פְּרִי לְמִינוֹ אֲשֶׁר זַרְעוֹ־
בוֹ עַל־הָאָרֶץ: וַיְהִי־כֵן: וַיַּרְא
אֱלֹהִים כִּי־טוֹב וַיְהִי־עֶרֶב
וַיְהִי־בֹקֶר יוֹם שְׁלִישִׁי: וַיֹּאמֶר
אֱלֹהִים יְהִי מְאֹרֹת בִּרְקִיעַ
הַשָּׁמַיִם לְהַבְדִּיל בֵּין הַיּוֹם
וּבֵין הַלָּיְלָה וְהָיוּ לְאֹתֹת
וּלְמוֹעֲדִים וּלְיָמִים וְשָׁנִים:
וְהָיוּ לִמְאוֹרֹת בִּרְקִיעַ הַשָּׁמַיִם

Let there be lights in the firmament of the heaven to divide the day
from the night; and let them be for signs, and for seasons, and for days
15 and for years: and let them be for lights in the firmament of the heaven

CRITICAL NOTES.

Creation: Higher Criticism presents i, 1-ii, 4, as a whole, untouched by a redactor's hand. Wellhausen, Kuenen, Kittel, Dillmann, Budde, Julicher, and their fol-
lowers, are unanimous in this verdict. This section is assigned by them to P, and
its date is given as about 450 B.C. The schools of Higher Criticism are quite as
unanimous in attributing ii, 4-25 to J; yet the hand of a redactor appears, and prin-
cipally in ii, 10-14. The concession is made, however, that "their formal charac-
teristics, style, and language, are identical." The earlier document J was written
about 800 B.C. Reconstructive Criticism regards the two chapters as composite,
made by uniting the Priestly Narrative with the Prophetical. This compositing
was done without redaction, simply by displacement. Higher Criticism demon-

CREATION.

2, 4 These are the generations of the heavens and the earth when they where created, in the day that Jehovah God made heaven and the
1, 2 earth. And the spirit of God moved upon the face of the wa-
7 ters. And God made the firmament, and divided the waters which were under the firmament from the waters which were above
16 the firmament. And God made two great lights; the greater light to rule the day, and the lesser light to rule the night: the stars
17 also. And God set them in the firmament of the heaven to give
18 light upon the earth, and to rule over the day and over the night, and to divide the light from the
21 darkness. And God created the great sea-monsters, and every living creature that moveth, which the waters brought forth abundantly, and every winged fowl
2, 3 after their kind, and every plant of the field before it was in the earth, and every herb of the field
1, 12 before it grew. And the earth brought forth grass, herb bearing seed after its kind, and the tree bearing fruit, wherein is the seed
25 thereof, after its kind. And God made the beast of the earth after its kind, and the cattle after its kind, and every thing that creepeth upon the ground after their
2, 6 kind. And there went up a mist from the earth and watered

אלה תולדות השמים והארץ
בהבראם ביום עשות יהוה
אלהים ארץ ושמים:ורוח
אלהים מרחפת על־פני־
המים:ויעש אלהים את־
הרקיע ויבדל בין המים
אשר מתחת לרקיע ובין
המים אשר מעל לרקיע:
ויעש אלהים את־שני המאת
הגדלים את־המאור הגדל
לממשלת היום ואת־המאור
הקטן לממשלת הלילה ואת
הכוכבים:ויתן אתם אלהים
ברקיע השמים להאיר על־
הארץ:ולמשול ביום
ובלילה והבדריל בין האור
ובין החשך:ויברא אלהים
את־התנינם הגדלים ואת
כל־נפש החיה הרמשת
אשר שרצו הים ואת כל־
עוף כנף למינהם:וכ ל־
שיח השרה שרם יהיר
בארץ וכל־עשב השדה
שרם יצמה:ויוצא הארץ
רשא עשב מזריע זרע
למינהו ועץ עשה־פרי
אשר זרעו־בו למינהו:ויעש
אלהים את־חית הארץ למינה
ואת־הבהמה למינה ות־כל־
רמש האדמה למינהם:ואד
יעלה מן־הארץ והשקה את־

CRITICAL NOTES.

strated two accounts of Creation. Yet in separating these two accounts, it proffers only records, which are contradictory; and indeed its second is but a partial one. Some scholars have been fond of characterizing the record of the second chapter as "picturesque," and that of the first as "precise." A whole string of epithets along this line have been unwound before our eyes. The important fact is, that the two accounts are essentially alike. There are in each six creative periods. The prophetic writer calls them days, in harmony with the mode of prophetic utterance in their prophecies. The priestly narrator simply states that God made all things, and the making is in a succession of six epochs. It does not characterize these epochs by any time-designations. At the close of the creative activity of God, both narratives are one in ascribing to the Creator a day of rest. The peculiar Hebrew

CREATION.

1, 18 to give light upon the earth: and it was so. And God saw that it
19 was good. And there was evening and there was morning, a fourth
20 day. And God said, Let the waters bring forth abundantly the moving creature that hath life, and let the fowl fly above the earth in the open firmament of the heaven,
21 after its kind: and it was so. And
22 God saw that it was good. And God blessed them, saying, Be fruitful, and multiply, and fill the waters in the seas, and let the fowl multiply
23 in the earth. And there was evening and there was morning, a fifth
24 day. And God said, Let the earth bring forth the living creature after its kind, cattle, and creeping things, and the beast of the earth after its
25 kind: and it was so. And God saw
26 that it was good. And God said, Let us make man in our own image, after our likeness: and let them have dominion over the fish of the sea, and over the fowl of the air, and over the cattle, and over all the earth, and over every creeping thing that creepeth upon the earth.
27 And God created man in his own image, in the image of God created he him; male and female created
28 he them. And God blessed them: and God said to them, Be fruitful, and multiply, and replenish the earth, and subdue it; and have dominion over the fish of the sea, and over the fowl of the air,
29 and over every living thing that moveth upon the earth. And God said, Behold, I have given you every herb yielding seed, which is

להאיר על־הארץ ויהי־כן
וירא אלהים כי־טוב: ויהי־
ערב ויהי־בקר יום רביעי:
ויאמר אלהים ישרצו המים
שרץ נפש חיה ועוף יעופף
על־הארץ על־פני רקיע
השמים למינהו: ויהי־כן
וירא אלהים כי־טוב: ויברך
אתם אלהים לאמר פרו
ורבו ומלאו את־המים בימים
והעוף ירב בארץ: ויהי־ערב
ויהי־בקר יום חמישי: ויאמר
אלהים תוצא הארץ נפש
חיה למינה בהמה ורמש
וחיתו ארץ למינה: ויהי־כן
וירא אלהים כי־טוב: ויאמר
אלהים נעשה אדם בצלמנו
כדמותנו וירדו בדגת הים
ובעוף השמים ובבהמה ובכל־
הארץ ובכל־הרמש הרמש
על־הארץ: ויברא אלהים
את־האדם בצלמו בצלם
אלהים ברא אתו זכר ונקבה
ברא אתם: ויברך אתם אלהים
ויאמר להם אלהים פרו
ורבו ומלאו את־הארץ
וכבשוה ורדו בדגת הים
ובעוף השמים ובכל־חיה
הרמשת על־הארץ: ויאמר
אלהים הנה נתתי לכם את־
כל־עשב זרע זרע אשר

CRITICAL NOTES.

sentences in ii, 2, 3, have arrested the attention of scholars often. The disentanglement of Reconstructive Criticism is shown above. It is a critical question, whether the word "day" does not belong simply to the Prophetical Narrative. But, at present, reasons seem to favor that it is common to both. Probably no factor has been more conspicuous in all the essays of Higher Criticism into the field opened by Genesis, than the divine names. Their presence or absence determines documents, redactors, and what not. Reconstructive Criticism asserts that Elohim marks through Genesis the Prophetic Narrative, and that Yehowah Elohim, or Elohim, is present in the Priestly Narrative. It is conceded that the displacement of these names

CREATION.

the whole face of the ground: for
2, 5 Jehovah God had not caused it to
rain upon the earth, and there was
7 no man to till the ground. And
Jehovah God formed man of the
dust of the ground, and breathed
into his nostrils the breath of life;
8 and man became a living soul. And
Jehovah God planted a garden east-
ward, in Eden; and there he put
the man whom he had formed.
9 And Jehovah God made to grow
out of the ground every tree that
is pleasant to the sight, and good
for food; and the tree of life in the
midst of the garden, and the tree
of the knowledge of good and evil.
10 And a river went out of Eden to water the garden; and from thence it
was parted, and became four heads.
11 The name of the first is Pishon;
that is it which compasseth the
whole land of Havilah, where there
12 is gold; and the gold of that land
is good: there is bdellium and onyx
13 stone. And the name of the second river is Gihon: the same is it
that compasseth the whole land of
14 Cush. And the name of the third
river is Hiddekel: that is it which
goeth in front of Assyria. And the
15 fourth river is Euphrates. And Jehovah God took the man, and put
him into the garden of Eden to
16 dress it and to keep it. And Jehovah God commanded the man, say-
17 ing, Of every tree of the garden thou mayest freely eat: but of the
tree of knowledge of good and evil, thou shalt not eat of it:

כָּל־פְּנֵי הָאֲדָמָה כִּי־ לֹא
הִמְטִיר יְהוָה אֱלֹהִים עַל־
הָאָרֶץ וְאָדָם אַיִן לַעֲבֹד אֶת־
הָאֲדָמָה:וַיִּצֶר יְהוָה אֱלֹהִים
אֶת־הָאָדָם עָפָר מִן הָאֲדָמָה
וַיִּפַּח בְּאַפָּיו נִשְׁמַת חַיִּים
וַיְהִי הָאָדָם לְנֶפֶשׁ חַיָּה:
וַיִּטַּע יְהוָה אֱלֹהִים גַּן בְּעֵדֶן
מִקֶּדֶם וַיָּשֶׂם שָׁם אֶת־הָאָדָם
אֲשֶׁר יָצָר: וַיַּצְמַח יְהוָה
אֱלֹהִים מִן־הָאֲדָמָה כָּל־עֵץ
נֶחְמָד לְמַרְאֶה, וְטוֹב לְמַאֲכָל
וְעֵץ הַחַיִּים בְּתוֹךְ הַגָּן וְעֵץ
הַדַּעַת טוֹב וָרָע:וְנָהָר יֹצֵא
מֵעֵדֶן לְהַשְׁקוֹת אֶת־הַגָּן וּמִשָּׁם
יִפָּרֵד וְהָיָה לְאַרְבָּעָה רָאשִׁים:
שֵׁם הָאֶחָד פִּישׁוֹן הוּא הַסֹּבֵב
אֵת־כָּל־אֶרֶץ הַחֲוִילָה אֲשֶׁר־
שָׁם הַזָּהָב:וּזְהַב הָאָרֶץ הַהוּא
טוֹב שָׁם הַבְּדֹלַח וְאֶבֶן
הַשֹּׁהַם:וְשֵׁם הַנָּהָר הַשֵּׁנִי
גִּיחוֹן הוּא הַסּוֹבֵב אֵת כָּל־אֶרֶץ
כּוּשׁ:וְשֵׁם הַנָּהָר הַשְּׁלִישִׁי
חִדֶּקֶל הוּא הַהֹלֵךְ קִדְמַת
אַשּׁוּר וְהַנָּהָר הָרְבִיעִי הוּא
פְרָת:וַיִּקַּח יְהוָה אֱלֹהִים אֶת־
הָאָדָם וַיַּנִּחֵהוּ בְגַן־עֵדֶן לְעָבְדָהּ
וּלְשָׁמְרָהּ:וַיְצַו יְהוָה אֱלֹהִים
עַל־הָאָדָם לֵאמֹר מִכֹּל עֵץ־
הַגָּן אָכֹל תֹּאכֵל:וּמֵעֵץ הַדַּעַת
טוֹב וָרָע לֹא תֹאכַל מִמֶּנּוּ

CRITICAL NOTES.

later has wrought confusion dire; and therefore these names have been the tor-
mentors of Higher Criticism. This, however, is a fact, these names were left in
their original places untouched in these first two chapters. It is very evident that
the prophetic account is dominated by a feeling every way different from that
found in the priestly. The "Word of God" is the power with the prophetic
spirit; while the "Work of Jehovah" is the admiration of the priestly eyes. The
prophetic spirit discerns that all the works of God are good; the priestly gaze is
poetic, seeing God as making two great lights; the greater to rule the day, the
lesser to rule the night. The priestly narrator emphasizes distinctions. Yet ever he
is full of feeling, gladly saying, "And he made the stars also." The prophetic nar-

CREATION.

upon the face of all the earth, and every tree, in which is the fruit of a tree yielding seed; to you it shall
1, 30 be for meat: and to every beast of the earth, and to every fowl of the air, and to every thing that creepeth upon the earth, wherein there is life, every green herb for
2, 20 meat: and it was so. And the man gave names to all the cattle, and to the fowl of the air, and to every
1, 31 beast of the field. And God saw everything which he had made, and, behold, it was very good. And there was evening and there was
2, 1 morning, the sixth day. And the heavens and the earth were fin-
2 ished, and all their hosts. And God rested on the seventh day from all
3 his work. And he blessed the seventh day, and hallowed it, because in it he rested from all his work, which God had created.

עַל־פְּנֵי כָל־הָאָרֶץ וְאֶת־כָּל־
הָעֵץ אֲשֶׁר בּוֹ פְרִי עֵץ זֹרֵעַ
זֶרַע לָכֶם יִהְיֶה לְאָכְלָה׃וּלְכָל־
חַיַּת הָאָרֶץ וּלְכָל־עוֹף הַשָּׁמַיִם
וּלְכֹל־רוֹמֵשׂ עַל־הָאָרֶץ אֲשֶׁר־
בּוֹ נֶפֶשׁ חַיָּה אֶת־כָּל־יֶרֶק
עֵשֶׂב לְאָכְלָה וַיְהִי־כֵן
וַיִּקְרָא הָאָדָם שֵׁמוֹת לְכֹל־
הַבְּהֵמָה וּלְעוֹף הַשָּׁמַיִם וּלְכָל־
חַיַּת הַשָּׂדֶה:וַיַּרְא אֱלֹהִים אֶת־
כָּל־אֲשֶׁר עָשָׂה וְהִנֵּה טוֹב ׃
מְאֹד:וַיְהִי־עֶרֶב וַיְהִי־בֹקֶר יוֹם
הַשִּׁשִּׁי׃וַיְכֻלּוּ הַשָּׁמַיִם וְהָאָרֶץ
וְכֹל צְבָאָם:וַיִּשְׁבֹּת אֱלֹהִים
בַּיּוֹם הַשְּׁבִיעִי מִכָּל־מְלַאכְתּוֹ
וַיְבָרֶךְ אֶת־יוֹם הַשְּׁבִיעִי וַיְקַדֵּשׁ
אֹתוֹ כִּי־בוֹ שָׁבַת מִכָּל־מְלַאכְתּוֹ
אֲשֶׁר בָּרָא אֱלֹהִים:

CRITICAL NOTES.

rator tells us that God created man in his own image. Man from this standpoint must effect good works, or else be at variance with his Creator. The priestly view beholds God in great care for man; for God makes him a help meet; plants for him a garden; gives him warning. God also punishes without hindrance disobedience. And this God is Jehovah, giving promise to man. The priestly writer is careful to preserve the great traditions of the earliest times, seeing in them helpful lessons for men; while these are gone over in silence by the prophetic spirit. Three great truths are for the prophet in creation: the power of God's word, his works all good, man in God's image. The priestly and prophetic view are at heart one, otherwise diverse. Different are these narratives in their use of the divine names,

CREATION.

for in the day that thou eatest
1, *18* thereof, thou shalt surely die. And
Jehovah God said, It is not good
that the man should be alone; I
will make him a help meet for
19 him. And out of the ground Jehovah God formed every beast of
the field, and every fowl of the
air; and he brought them unto the
man to see what he would call
them: and whatsoever the man
called every living creature, that
20 was the name thereof. But for
man there was not found a help
21 meet for him. And Jehovah God
caused a deep sleep to fall upon
the man, and he slept; and he took
one of his ribs, and closed up the
22 flesh instead thereof: and the rib,
which Jehovah God had taken
from man, made he a woman, and
23 brought to the man. And the
man said, This is now bone of my
bones, and flesh of my flesh: she
shall be called Woman, because she
24 was taken out of Man. Therefore
shall a man leave his father and
his mother, and shall cleave unto
his wife: and they shall be one
25 flesh. And they were both naked,
the man and his wife, and were
2, *2* not ashamed. And God finished
on the seventh day to do all the
work which he had made. And he

כִּי בְּיוֹם אֲכָלְךָ מִמֶּנּוּ מוֹת
תָּמוּת:וַיֹּאמֶר יְהוָה אֱלֹהִים
לֹא־טוֹב הֱיוֹת הָאָדָם לְבַדּוֹ
אֶעֱשֶׂה־לּוֹ עֵזֶר כְּנֶגְדּוֹ:
וַיִּצֶר יְהוָה אֱלֹהִים מִן־
הָאֲדָמָה כָּל־חַיַּת הַשָּׂדֶה
וְאֵת כָּל־עוֹף הַשָּׁמַיִם וַיָּבֵא
אֶל־הָאָדָם לִרְאוֹת מַה־
יִּקְרָא־לוֹ וְכֹל אֲשֶׁר יִקְרָא
לּוֹ הָאָדָם נֶפֶשׁ חַיָּה הוּא
שְׁמוֹ:וּלְאָדָם לֹא־מָצָא עֵזֶר
כְּנֶגְדּוֹ:וַיַּפֵּל יְהוָה אֱלֹהִים תַּרְדֵּמָה
עַל־הָאָדָם וַיִּישָׁן וַיִּקַּח אַחַת
מִצַּלְעֹתָיו וַיִּסְגֹּר בָּשָׂר תַּחְתֶּנָּה:
וַיִּבֶן יְהוָה אֱלֹהִים אֶת־הַצֵּלָע
אֲשֶׁר לָקַח מִן־הָאָדָם לְאִשָּׁה
וַיְבִאֶהָ אֶל־הָאָדָם; וַיֹּאמֶר
הָאָדָם זֹאת הַפַּעַם עֶצֶם
מֵעֲצָמַי וּבָשָׂר מִבְּשָׂרִי
לְזֹאת יִקָּרֵא אִשָּׁה כִּי מֵאִישׁ
לֻקֳחָה זֹּאת:עַל־כֵּן יַעֲזָב
אִישׁ אֶת־אָבִיו וְאֶת־אִמּוֹ
וְדָבַק בְּאִשְׁתּוֹ וְהָיוּ לְבָשָׂר
אֶחָד:וַיִּהְיוּ שְׁנֵיהֶם עֲרוּמִּים
הָאָדָם וְאִשְׁתּוֹ וְלֹא יִתְבֹּשָׁשׁוּ:
וַיְכַל אֱלֹהִים בַּיּוֹם הַשְּׁבִיעִי
לַעֲשׂוֹת מְלַאכְתּוֹ אֲשֶׁר עָשָׂה:
וַיִּשְׁבֹּת בַּיּוֹם הַשְּׁבִיעִי וַיְבָרֶךְ
אֱלֹהִים אֶת־יוֹם הַשְּׁבִיעִי
וַיְקַדֵּשׁ אֹתוֹ כִּי בוֹ שָׁבַת מִכָּל־
מְלַאכְתּוֹ אֲשֶׁר עָשָׂה:

3 rested on the seventh day. And God blessed the seventh day, and
hallowed it, because in it he rested from all the work which he had
made.

CRITICAL NOTES.

in the literary form which is employed to give expression to the common facts,
and in the instruction to be derived from the recorded events. With the prophet
mind God is our Creator, with the priestly mind Jehovah is our Maker.

TEMPTATION AND FALL.

3, 1 Now the serpent was more subtil than any beast of the field which Jehovah God had made. And he said unto the woman, Yea, hath God said, Ye shall not eat of any tree 2 of the garden? And the woman said unto the serpent, Of the fruit of the 3 trees of the garden we may eat: but of the fruit of the tree which is in the midst of the garden, God hath said, Ye shall not eat of it, neither 4 shall ye touch it, lest ye die. And the serpent said unto the woman, Ye 5 shall not surely die: for God doth know that in the day ye eat there-6 of, then your eyes shall be opened and ye shall be as gods, knowing good and evil. And when the woman saw that the tree was good for food, and that it was a delight to the eyes, and that the tree was to be desired to make one wise, she took of the fruit thereof, and did eat; and she gave also unto her husband 7 with her, and he did eat. And the eyes of them both were opened, and they knew that they were naked; and they sewed fig leaves together, and made themselves aprons.

THE ANNOUNCEMENT OF THE CURSE.

3, 8 And they heard the voice of Jehovah God who was walking in the garden in the cool of the day: and the man and his wife hid themselves from the presence of Jehovah God amongst the trees of 9 the garden. And Jehovah God called unto the man, and said

ונחש היה ערום מכל חית
השדה אשר עשה יהוה
אלהים ויאמר אל האשה
אף כי־אמר אלהים לא
תאכלו מכל עץ הגן:
ותאמר האשה אל־הנחש
מפרי עץ־הגן נאכל:ומפרי
העץ אשר בתוך־הגן אמר
אלהים לא תאכלו ממנו ולא
תגעו בו פן תמתון: ויאמר
הנחש אל־האשה לא מות
תמתון: כי ירה אלהים כי
ביום אכלכם ממנו ונפקחו
עיניכם והייתם כאלהי
ירעי טוב ורע:ותרא
האשה כי טוב העץ למאכל
וכי תאוה־הוא לעינים
ונחמד העץ להשכיל ותקח
מפריו ותאכל ותתן גם
לאישה עמה ויאכל:ותפקחנה
עיני שניהם וידעו כי עירמם
הם ויתפרו עלה תאנה
ויעשו להם הגרת:

וישמעו את־קול יהוה אלהים
מתהלך בגן לרוח היום
ויתחבא האדם ואשתו
מפני יהוה אלהים בתוך
עץ הגן:ויקרא יהוה
אלהים אל־האדם ויאמר

CRITICAL NOTES.

Temptation and Fall: Higher Criticism assigns Section 3, 1-7, to J, a writer of about 800 B. C. Reconstructive Criticism places it in the Priestly Narrative. Agreement is in finding but one author for this passage. The narrative is a continuation of the life in Eden. The episode has God's command as central. The fall is due to temptation. Falling is disobedience to the command of Jehovah. Tradition, in the Hebrew nation, asserts a personal tempter in the form of a serpent. Adam's knowledge, gained by disobedience, wrought confusion, increased cares. This lesson is what made the tradition precious to the priestly narrator according to Reconstructive Criticism. The lesson was gold in the ore. He therefore retains it in his work.

THE ANNOUNCEMENT OF THE CURSE.

3, 10 unto him. Where art thou? And he said, I heard thy voice in the garden, and I was afraid, because I **11** was naked; and I hid myself. And he said, Who told thee that thou wast naked? Hast thou eaten of the tree, whereof I commanded thee **12** that thou shouldst not eat? And the man said, The woman whom thou gavest to be with me, she gave me of the tree, and I did eat. **13** And Jehovah God said unto the woman, What is this thou hast done? And the woman said, The serpent beguiled me, and I did eat. **14** And Jehovah God said unto the serpent, Because thou hast done this, cursed art thou above all cattle, and above every beast of the field; thou who goest upon thy belly, and eatest **15** dust all thy days: verily I will put enmity between thee and the woman, and between thy seed and her seed: it shall bruise thy head, and thou shalt bruise his heel. **16** Unto the woman he said. I will greatly multiply thy sorrow and thy conception; in sorrow thou shalt bring forth children; and thy desire shall be unto thy husband, **17** and he shall rule over thee. And unto Adam he said, Because thou hast hearkened unto the voice of thy wife, and hast eaten of the tree, of which

לו איכה:ויאטר את־קולך
שמעתי בגן ואירא לי־עירם
אנכי ואחבא:ויאמר מי הגיד
לך כי עירם אחח המן־העץ
אשר צויתיך לבלתי אכל׳
ממנו אכלת:ויאטר האדם
האשה אשר נתח עטדי
הוא נתנה־לי טן־העץ
ואכל:ויאמר יהוה אלהים
לאשה מה־זאת עשי.ת
ותאמר האשה הנחש השאני
ואכל:ויאמר יהוה אלהי
אל־הנחש כי עשית זאת
ארור אתה מכל־הבהמה
ועכל הית השרה על־
גחנך תלך ועפר תאכל כל
כל־ יטי חייך:ואיבה אשית
בינך ובין האשה ובין
זרעך ובין זדעה הוא ישופך
ראש ואתה חושופנו עקב׳.
אל־האשה אמר הרבי
ארבה עצבונך והרנך
בעצב תלדי בנים ואל־
אשך תשוקחך והוא ימשל־
בך:ולאדם אמר כי שמעת
לקיל אשתך ותאכל טן־
עץ אשר צויתיך לאמר לא
תאכל טמנו ארורה הארטה
בעבורך בעצבון תאכלנך
כל יטי חייך:וקוץ ודרדב
תצמיח לך ואכלת את־

I commanded thee, saying, Thou shalt not eat of it: cursed is the ground **18** for thy sake; in toil shalt thou eat of it all the days of thy life; thorns **19** also and thistles shall it bring forth to thee; yet thou shalt eat the

CRITICAL NOTES.

The Announcement of the Curse: Section 3, 8-19, a narrative of J according to Higher Criticism. The significance of this admission for Reconstructive Criticism is simply that this portion is by concession from a single writer. Our priestly writer records the conduct of Jehovah God toward all connected with the First Transgression. Was ever tradition freighted with profounder truth for mankind? The Tempter is an object of loathing because of the form he assumed, is condemned to defeat; the woman is assigned to the realm of pains and subjection; the man is made a toiler for food in the earth, which was become hostile to his labor. The prophetic writer passes by the tradition of Eden; but he will declare again and again that punishment is indissolubly connected with disobedience to God.

GENERATIONS OF ADAM.

5. 3   And Adam lived an hundred and
thirty years and begat in his own
likeness, after his own image, and
4 called his name Seth. And the
days of Adam after he begat Seth
were eight hundred years: and he
6 begat sons and daughters. And
Seth lived an hundred and five
7 years, and begat Enosh: And Seth

וייחי אדם שלשש ומאת שנה
וייולד בדמתה כצלמו ויקרא
את־שמו שת: וייחי ימי-אדם
אחרי הולירו את־שת שמנה
מאת שנה ויולד בנים ובנת:
ויחי־שת חמש שנים ומאת
שנה ויולד את־אנוש: ויחי־
שת אחרי הולירו את־אנוש שבע
שנים ושמנה מאת שנה ויולד

lived after he begat Enosh eight hundred and seven years, and begat

CRITICAL NOTES.

Generations of Adam : Reconstructive Criticism separates this composite account into
the two original tables. The writer of the Prophetic Narrative selects simply the
Sethite lineal representative of each family, tells the age of the parent at the time of
the birth of this family representative, and the number of years which the parent
lived afterwards, concluding with the statement that other children, sons and
daughters, were born. The writer of the Priestly Narrative enumerates three
male children of Adam, recounts the fate of Abel, mentions the descendants of
Cain, and also those of Seth, giving the ages only of the Sethite representatives,
and concluding with the expression, "and he died." Each table has its own
peculiar and distinctive character. These Genealogies (iv. 17-v. 31), according to
Higher Criticism, show most remarkable redactions as well as authorship; iv. 1, is

THE ANNOUNCEMENT OF THE CURSE.

3, 19 herb of the field; in the sweat of thy brow thou shalt eat the food, till thou return unto the ground; for out of it wast thou taken: for dust thou art, and unto dust shalt thou return

עשה השדה׃בזעת אפיך
תאכל לחם עד שובך אל-
האדמה כי ממנה לקחת׃
כי-עפר אתה ואל-עפר
תשוב׃

EXPULSION FROM EDEN.

3, 21 And Jehovah God made for Adam and for his wife coats of skins, and 22 clothed them. And Jehovah God said, Behold, the man is become as one of us, to know good and evil; and now, lest he put forth his hand, and take also of the tree of life, and 23 eat, and live forever: surely Jehovah God shall send him forth from the garden of Eden to till the ground from whence he was taken. 24 And he drove out the man; and placed at the east of the garden of Eden the Cherubim, and the flame of a sword which turned every way, to keep the way of the tree of life.

ויעש יהוה אלהים לאדם
ולאשתו כתנות עור וילבשם׃
ויאמר יהוה אלהים הן האדם
היה כאחד ממנו לדעת טוב
ורע ועתה פן־ישלח ידו ולקח
גם מעץ החיים ואכל וחי
לעלם׃וישלחהו יהוה אלהים
מגן־עדן לעבד את־האדמה
אשר לקח משם׃ ויגרש את־
האדם וישכן מקדם לגן־עדן
את־הכרבים ואת להט החרב
המתהפכת לשמר את־דרך
עץ החיים׃

GENERATIONS OF ADAM.

5, 1 This is the book of the genera- tions of Adam. In the day that God created man, when he made 2 him in the likeness of God. He created them male and female; and blessed them, and called their name Adam, in the day when they 3, 20 were created. And the man called

זה ספר תולרות אדם ביום
ברא אלהים אדם בדמות
אלהים עשה אתו׃ זכר
ונקבה בראם ויברך אתם
ויקרא את־שמם אדם ביום
הבראם׃ויקרא האדם שם
אשתו חוה כי הוא היתה
אם כל־חי׃והאדם ידע
את־חוה אשתו ותהר ותלר

4, 1 his wife's name Eve, because she was the mother of all living. And the man knew Eve, his wife; and she conceived and bare

CRITICAL NOTES.

Expulsion from Eden: Section 3, 21-24, concludes all that the priestly writer associates with the earliest life of man. Christian writers designate the episode as the Expulsion from Eden. Higher Criticism finds here two writers, J and his redactor J². This dual authorship accounts for the supposed " conflicting reasons " (cf. v. 23 with vv. 22 and 24) given for the expulsion from Eden. Our priestly nar- rative has no conflict of reasons ; but sees here the penalty of disobedience, which was death, inflicted by loss of Eden and so of access to the Tree of Life.

Generations of Adam—Continued: J ; 2-16 is J² ; 16-24 is J ; 25-26 is J² ; v, 1-28. is P ; 29 is J ; 30-32 is P. It is quite apparent that the solution of Higher Criticism proffers little help. The document P was written about 150 B. C., and is separated

GENERATIONS OF ADAM.

6, 10 sons and daughters. And Enosh lived ninety years, and begat Kenan. And Enosh lived after he begat Kenan eight hundred and fifteen years, and begat sons and daugh-
12 ters. And Kenan lived seventy
13 years, and begat Mahalalel: and Kenan lived after he begat Mahalalel eight hundred and forty years,
15 and begat sons and daughters. And Mahalalel lived sixty-five years and
16 begat Jared. And Mahalalel lived after he begat Jared eight hundred and thirty years, and begat sons
18 and daughters. And Jared lived an hundred sixty and two years,
19 and begat Enoch. And Jared lived after he begat Enoch eight hundred years, and begat sons and
21 daughters. And Enoch lived sixty and five years, and begat Methuse-
22 lah. And Enoch walked with God after he begat Methuselah three hundred years, and begat sons and
₇ daughters. And Methuselah lived an hundred eighty and seven years,
26 and begat Lamech. And Methuselah lived after he begat Lamech seven hundred eighty and two years, and begat sons and daugh-
28 ters. And Lamech lived an hundred eighty and two years, and
30 begat Noah. And Lamech lived after he begat Noah five hundred ninety and five years, and

בנים ובנות:ויחי אנוש תשעים
שנה ויולד את־קינן:ויחי אנוש
אחרי הולידו את־ק׳נן וחמשׁ
עמדע שנה ושמנה מצוהת שנה
ויולד בנים ובנות ידיחי־ קינן
שבעים שנה ויולד את־מהללאל:
ויחי היכן אחרי הולידו את־
מהללאל ארבעׁת שנה ושמנה
מאות שנה ויולד בנים ובנות:
ויהי הללאל חמש ע׳נים וששׁ
שנה ויולד את־ירד:ויחי
מהללאל אחרי הולידו את־ירד
שלשים שנה ושמנה מאות
שנה ויולד בנים ובנות:ויחי־
ירד שתים ושׁשׁים ׳שנה ומאת
שנה ויולד את־חנון׃:ויחי־ירד
אחרי הולידו את־חנוך שׁמנה
מאות שנה ויולד בנים ובנות:ויחי־
חנוך חמש וששׁים שנה ויולד
את־ מתושלח:ויתהלך חנוך את־
האלהים אחרי הולידו את־מתושלח
שלש מאות שנה ויולד בני ם
ובנות:ויחי מתושאל שבע ושׁמׁנׁים
שנה ומאת שנה ויולד את לסך.
ויחי מתושלח אחרי הולידו את־
למך. שתים ושׁמנים שנה ושבע
מאות שנה ויולד בנים ובנות:
יחי־למך שתׁי׳ג ושמנׁים שנה
ומאת שנה ויולד את־נח:ויחי
למך אחרי הולידו את־נח חמש
ותשׁעׁ ים שנה וחמש מאת שנה
ויוכד בנים ובנות׃

he begat sons and daughters.

CRITICAL NOTES.

from the earlier document J by at least three centuries and a half. Then, too, J is supplemented by J². What credence will genealogical tables, thus constructed, win from the reader? But, nevertheless, Higher Criticism emphasized the incongruities in the account of these genealogies, and prepared the way for their removal. The Prophetic Narrative of Reconstructive Criticism departs from its formula in but two instances : it states of Adam that he begat "in his own likeness, after his own image;" it states of Enoch, that "he walked with God." The prophetic writer passes down through centuries and makes no comment, except that the son had the image and likeness of the parent. In sad silence he contemplates his knowledge of the representatives of families, until he reaches Enoch, when he speaks, saying that Enoch walked with God. The priestly writer, on the contrary, records tra-

GENERATIONS OF ADAM.

Cain, and said, I have gotten a man
4, 2 with the help of Jehovah. And
again she bare his brother Abel.

THE ACCEPTED OFFERING.

4, 2 And Abel was a keeper of sheep,
but Cain was a tiller of the ground.
3 And in process of time it came to
pass, that Cain brought of the fruit
of the ground an offering to Jeho-
4 vah. And Abel, he also brought of
the firstlings of his flock and of the
fat thereof. And Jehovah had respect unto Abel and to his offering;
5 but unto Cain and to his offering
he had not respect. And Cain was
very wroth, and his countenance
6 fell. And Jehovah said unto Cain,
Why art thou wroth? And why is
7 thy countenance fallen? If thou
doest well, shalt thou not be accepted? And if thou doest not
well, sin coucheth at the door: and
desire of it is thine; but thou mayest rule over it. And Cain told
this to Abel his brother.

THE MURDER OF ABEL.

4, 8 And it came to pass, when they
were in the field, that Cain rose up
against Abel his brother, and slew
9 him. And Jehovah said unto Cain,
Where is Abel thy brother? And
he said, I know not: am I my
10 brother's keeper? And he said, What hast thou done? the voice of
11 thy brother's blood crieth unto me from the ground. And now
cursed art thou more than the ground, which hath opened her mouth
12 to receive thy brother's blood from thy hand; when thou tilledst

את־קין ותאמר קניתי איש
את־יהוה:ותסף ללרת את־
אחיו את־הבל:

ויהי־הבל רעה צאן וקין היה
עבר אדמה:ויהי־מקץ ימים
ויבא קין מפרי האדמה
מנחה ליהוה:והבל הביא גם־הוא
מבכרת צאנו ומחלבהם
וישע יהוה אל־הבל ואל־
מנחתו:ואל־קין ואל־מנחתו
לא שעה ויחר לקין מאד־
ויפלו פניו:ויאמר יהוה אל־
קין למה חרה לך ולמה כפלו
פניך:הלוא אם־תיטיב שאת
ואם לא תיטיב לפתח חטאת
רבץ ואליך תשוקתו ואתה
תמשל־בו:ויאמר קין אל־
הבל אחיו:

ויהי בהיותם בשרה ויהם קין
אל־הבל אחיו ויהרגהו:ויאמר
יהוה אל־קין אי הבל אחיך ויאמר
לא ידעתי השמר אחי אנכי:
ויאמר מה עשת קול דמי
אחיך צעקים אלי מן האדמה:
ועתה ארור אתה סן־האדמה
אשר פצתה את־פיה לקחת
את־דמי אחיך מידך:כי תעבר

CRITICAL NOTES.

ditions connected with these families; not alone the Sethites, but also Cainites.
The birth of Cain, in the priestly narrative, leads Eve to acknowledge Jehovah.

Accepted Offering and the Murder of Abel: It is to be noticed that the priestly
writer interrupts his account of the Generations of Adam with these two early
traditions. The literary form of the narrative is similar to that employed in the
narrative of the Garden of Eden. Jehovah talks with Cain as he talked with Adam
and Eve in the garden. Jehovah decrees punishment by word of mouth to Cain
the same as he did to Adam and Eve. These facts indicate unity of authorship.

CRITICAL NOTES.

The priestly narrator gives first the descendants of Cain. Incident is interwoven with the account. Cain calls a city after the name his own son had received. Lamech's family are noted for their work in iron and brass, for the graver and the musician. Lamech himself, violent like Cain, murders, and vaunts security beyond Cain as much more as his violence was vaster. Enoch walked with God, and "God took him." The Priestly Narrative is dominated by one actuating mind, permeated by one prevailing religious faith in Jehovah. The oneness of the Priestly Narrative is indicated in the words which speak of the reason for the naming of Noah: "This one shall comfort us after our work and the toil of our hands, because of the ground which Jehovah God hath cursed." Thus appears a witness to the curse placed upon the ground because Adam transgressed.

THE MURDER OF ABEL.

the ground, it gave not its strength to thee; a fugitive and a wanderer

i, 13 shalt thou be in the earth. And Cain said unto Jehovah, My punishment is greater than I can bear.

14 Behold, thou hast driven me from the face of the ground; and I shall be hidden from thy face; and shall be a fugitive and a wanderer in the earth; and it shall come to pass, that whosoever findeth me shall

15 slay me. And Jehovah said unto him, Therefore whosoever slayeth Cain, vengeance shall be taken on him sevenfold. And Jehovah appointed a sign for Cain, lest any finding him should smite him.

16 And Cain went out from the presence of Jehovah, and dwelt in the land of Nod, on the east of Eden.

GENERATIONS OF ADAM.

[CONTINUED.]

4, 25 And Adam knew again his wife; and she bare a son, and called his name Seth: for God hath appointed me another seed instead of Abel;

5, 3 for Cain slew him. And all the days that Adam lived were nine hundred and thirty years: and he

4, 17 died. And Cain knew his wife: and she conceived, and bare Enoch; and he builded a city, and called the name of the city, by the name

18 of his son, Enoch. And unto Enoch was born Irad: and Irad begat Mehujael: and Mehujael begat Methushael: and Methu-

19 shael begat Lamech. And Lamech took unto him two wives: the name of the one was Adah, and the name of the other Zil-

20 lah. And Adah bare Jabal: he was the father of such as dwell

אֶת־הָאֲדָמָה לֹא־תֹסֵף תֵּת־כֹּחָהּ
כָּחָהּ לָךְ נָע וָנָד תִּהְיֶה בָאָרֶץ:
וַיֹּאמֶר לוֹ אֶל־יְהוָה גָּדוֹל
עֲוֹנִי מִנְּשׂוֹא: הֵן גֵּרַשְׁתָּ אֹתִי
הַיּוֹם מֵעַל פְּנֵי הָאֲדָמָה וּמִפָּנֶיךָ
אֶסָּתֵר וְהָיִיתִי נָע וָנָד בָּאָרֶץ
וְהָיָה כָל־מֹצְאִי יַהַרְגֵנִי:
וַיֹּאמֶר לוֹ יְהוָה לָכֵן כָּל־
הֹרֵג קַיִן שִׁבְעָתַיִם יֻקָּם
וַיָּשֶׂם יְהוָה לְקַיִן אוֹת לְבִלְתִּי
הַכּוֹת אֹתוֹ כָל־מֹצְאוֹ וַיֵּצֵא
קַיִן מִלִּפְנֵי יְהוָה וַיֵּשֶׁב בְּאֶרֶץ
נוֹד קִדְמַת־עֵדֶן:

וַיֵּדַע אָדָם עוֹד אֶת־אִשְׁתּוֹ
וַתֵּלֶד בֵּן וַתִּקְרָא אֶת־שְׁמוֹ שֵׁת
כִּי שָׁת־לִי אֱלֹהִים זֶרַע אַחֵר
תַּחַת הֶבֶל כִּי הֲרָגוֹ קָיִן:
וַיִּהְיוּ כָל־יְמֵי אָדָם אֲשֶׁר־חַי
תְּשַׁע מֵאוֹת שָׁנָה וּשְׁלֹשִׁים שָׁנָה
וַיָּמֹת: וַיֵּדַע קַיִן אֶת־אִשְׁתּוֹ
וַתַּהַר וַתֵּלֶד אֶת־חֲנוֹךְ וַיְהִי בֹנֶה
עִיר וַיִּקְרָא שֵׁם הָעִיר כְּשֵׁם
בְּנוֹ חֲנוֹךְ: וַיִּוָּלֵד לַחֲנוֹךְ אֶת־עִירָד
וְעִירָד יָלַד אֶת־מְחוּיָאֵל וּמְחוּיָאֵל
יָלַד אֶת־מְתוּשָׁאֵל וּמְתוּשָׁאֵל
יָלַד אֶת־לָמֶךְ: וַיִּקַּח־לוֹ לֶמֶךְ
שְׁתֵּי נָשִׁים שֵׁם הָאַחַת עָדָה
וְשֵׁם הַשֵּׁנִית צִלָּה: וַתֵּלֶד עָדָה
אֶת־יָבָל הוּא הָיָה אֲבִי יֹשֵׁב

CRITICAL NOTES.

Generations of Adam—Continued : It is to be noticed that Higher Criticism concedes iv, 2-16, to be "obviously connected" with chapter iii, an early supplementation in a similar style. It holds also that the proud boast of security (v. 24), which Lamech makes, is older than Jehovah's assurance to Cain, that vengeance would be taken sevenfold upon any one who should slay Cain. Reconstructive Criticism asserts identity of authorship for this section, and affirms priority of Jehovah's promise to Cain. The growth of wickedness in the descendants of Cain is fearfully depicted by the priestly writer, when he records that Lamech takes the promise of protection

CRITICAL NOTES.

to the almost crushed spirit of Cain, which Jehovah gave when he made known the punishment for the murder of Abel, and refers to it as warrant for high-handed violence such as murder for a wound, and murder for even a hurt. Higher Criticism assigns v, 1-28, to P. It recognizes "a regular formula" which the writer employs. Reconstructive Criticism points out two formulæ, which are combined in this passage: one belonging to the Priestly Narrative, the other to the Prophetic. These two formulæ will appear again. The peculiar statement concerning Enoch, twice made, is supposed to be due, according to Higher Criticism, "to data afforded by

GENERATIONS OF ADAM.

4, 21 in tents and cattle. And his brother's name was Jubal: he was the
father of all such as handle the
22 harp and pipe. And Zillah, she
also bare Tubal-cain, the forger of
every cutting instrument of brass
and iron: and the sister of Tubal-
23 cain was Naamah. And Lamech
said unto his wives:
　Adah and Zillah, hear my voice;
　Ye wives of Lamech, hearken un-
　　to my speech:
　For I slew a man for wounding
　　me,
　And a youth for hurting me:
24 For Cain had sevenfold venge-
　　ance,
　And Lamech seventy and seven-
　　fold.
26 And to Seth, to him also there was
born a son; and he called his name
Enosh: then men began to call
5, 8 upon the name of Jehovah. And
all the days of Seth were nine hundred and twelve years: and he
died. And Enosh begat Kenan:
11 and all the days of Enosh were
nine hundred and five years: and
he died. And Kenan begat Mahala-
14 lel: and all the days of Kenan were
nine hundred and ten years: and
he died. And Mahalalel begat Ja-
17 red: and all the days of Mahalalel
were eight hundred ninety - five
20 years: and he died. And Jared begat Enoch: and all the days
of Jared were nine hundred sixty and two years: and he died.
23 And Enoch begat Methuselah: and all the days of Enoch were three
24 hundred sixty and five years. And Enoch walked with God: and he
was not; for God took him. And Methuselah begat Lamech: and

CRITICAL NOTES.

the genealogy of the flood interpolator." Reconstructive Criticism finds the peculiar statement such an indissoluble characteristic of Enoch that neither of the two
writers, the prophetic nor the priestly, could avoid its mention. Yet the priestly,
not the prophetic writer, finds reason for asserting the translation of Enoch in the
words that "Enoch walked with God, and God took him."
　The substantial identity of these two writers, in their accounts of the Generations of Adam, needs no proof. Their independence is evidenced not alone by what
each records, but also by the style in which the records are kept. The prophetic

GENERATIONS OF NOAH.

5, 32   And Noah was five hundred years
        old : and Noah begat Shem, Ham,
6, 7   and Japheth. The Nephalim were
        in the earth in those days. And
11   the earth was corrupt before God,
        and the earth was filled with vio-
12   lence. And God saw the earth,
        and, behold, it was corrupt; for all
        flesh had corrupted his way upon
9   the earth. Noah walked with God.

ויהי־נח בן־חמש מאות שנה
ויולד נח את־שם את־חם
ואת־יפת:הנפלים היו בארץ
בימים ההם:ותשחת הארץ
לפני האלהים ותמלא הארץ
חמס:וירא אלהים את־הארץ
והנה נשחתה כי־השחית כל־
בשר את־דרכו על־הארץ:
את־האלהים התהלך נח:

CRITICAL NOTES.

writer, in his genealogies, has a more restricted view, confining himself to the
Sethite line. His interest is not in the doings of those who lived before Noah,
except in the single case of Enoch. The priestly writer seeks every indication of
knowledge of man as related to Jehovah in the antediluvian ages.

Generations of Noah: The Higher Critics assign vi, 1–8, to J and his redactors, and
9–12, to P. It is a strange medley under this view. The solution of the sections
according to Reconstructive Criticism presents two narratives in substantial agree-

GENERATIONS OF ADAM.

5, 27 all the days of Methuselah were nine hundred sixty and nine years: 28 and he died. And Lamech begat a son: and he called his name Noah, saying, This one shall comfort us after our work and the toil of our hands, because of the ground 31 which Jehovah hath cursed. And all the days of Lamech were seven hundred seventy and seven years: and he died.

כל-ימי מתושלח תשע ושׁתים שנה ותשע מאות שנה וימת׃ ולמך בן ויולד בשׁני נח לאמר זה ינחמנו ממעשנו ומ עצבון ידינו מן־האדמה אשׁר אררה יהוה׃ויהי כל-ימי-לםך שבע ושבעים שנה ושבע מאות שׁנה וימת׃

GENERATIONS OF NOAH.

6, 9 These are the generations of Noah. 10 And Noah begat three sons, Shem, 11 Ham, and Japhet. And it came to pass, when men began to multiply on the face of the ground, and daughters were born unto them, 2 that the sons of God saw the daughters of men that they were fair; and they took them wives of 4 all that they chose. And also afterward, when the sons of God came in unto the daughters of men, they bare children unto them: these were the mighty men, who were of 3 old, the men of renown. And Jehovah said, My spirit shall not strive with man for ever, for that he is flesh; and his days will become an hundred and twenty 5 years. Still Jehovah saw that the

אלה תולרת נח:ויולד נח שלשה בנים את-שם את-חם ואת-יפת:ויהי כי הח ל האדם לרב על-פני האדמה ובנות ילדו להם:וירׁאו בני- האלהים את-בנות האדם כי טבת הנה ויקחו להם נשׁים מכל אשׁר בחרו:וגם אחרי- כן אשׁר יבאו בני האלהים אל-בנות האדם וילדו להם: הנה הגברים אשׁר מעולם אנשי השם:ויׁאמר יהוה לא ידון רוחי באדם לעלם בשׁגם הוא בשׂר וחיו ימיו מאה ועשרים שׁנה: וירא יהוה כי רבה רעת האדם בארץ וכל-יצר מחשׁב ת לבו רק רע כל-היום:וינחם יהוה כי-עשה את-האדם ב ארץ ויתעצב אל- לבו : ויׁאמר יהוה אמחה את- האדם אשׁר בראתי מעל

wickedness of man was great in the earth, and that every imagination of the thoughts of his heart 6 was only evil continually. And it repented Jehovah, that he had 7 made man on the earth, and it grieved him at his heart. And Jehovah said, I will destroy the man whom I have created from

CRITICAL NOTES.

ment. The Prophetic Narrative is the briefer, it is most intense. The prophetic writer says, the Nephalim lived at that time, the earth was corrupt and filled with violence. He says, also, God saw it all. Noah alone of all men walked with God. The priestly writer records the same facts; but traditional incidents are interwoven with them. He also describes Jehovah as reasoning with himself, and purposing to destroy man and all flesh. The priestly style is most apparent

NOAH AND THE ARK.

6, *13* And God said unto Noah, The end of all flesh is come before me; for the earth is filled with violence through them; and, behold, I will *14* destroy them with the earth. Make for thee an ark of gopher wood; rooms shalt thou make in the ark, and shalt pitch it within and with-*16* out with pitch. A light shalt thou make to the ark, and the door of the ark shalt thou set in the side *17* thereof. And I, behold, I do bring the flood of waters upon the earth, to destroy all flesh, wherein is the breath of life, from under the *18* heaven. But thou shalt come into the ark, thou, and thy sons, and thy wife, and thy sons' wives with *19* thee. And of every living thing of all flesh, two of every sort shall come to the ark, to be kept alive with thee, male and female they *20* shall be. Of the fowl after their kind, and of the cattle after their kind, of every creeping thing of the ground after its kind, two of every sort, shall come unto thee to *21* be kept alive. And take thou unto thee of all food that is eaten, and gather it unto thee; and it shall be for food for thee, and for *22* them. Thus did Noah; according to all that God commanded him.

וַיֹּאמֶר אֱלֹהִים לְנֹחַ קֵץ כָּל־בָּשָׂר
בָּא לְפָנַי כִּי־מָלְאָה הָאָרֶץ חָמָס
מִפְּנֵיהֶם וְהִנְנִי מַשְׁחִיתָם אֶת־
הָאָרֶץ: עֲשֵׂה לְךָ תֵּבַת עֲצֵי־
גֹפֶר קִנִּים תַּעֲשֶׂה אֶת־הַתֵּבָה
וְכָפַרְתָּ אֹתָהּ מִבַּיִת וּמִחוּץ
בַּכֹּפֶר: צֹהַר תַּעֲשֶׂה לַתֵּבָה
וּפֶתַח הַתֵּבָה בְּצִדָּהּ תָּשִׂים:
וַאֲנִי הִנְנִי מֵבִיא אֶת־הַמַּבּוּל
מַיִם עַל־הָאָרֶץ לְשַׁחֵת כָּל־
בָּשָׂר אֲשֶׁר־בּוֹ רוּחַ חַיִּים
מִתַּחַת הַשָּׁמָיִם: וּבָאתָ אֶל־
הַתֵּבָה אַתָּה וּבָנֶיךָ וְאִשְׁתְּךָ
וּנְשֵׁי־בָנֶיךָ אִתָּךְ: וּמִכָּל־הָחַי
מִכָּל־בָּשָׂר שְׁנַיִם מִכֹּל תָּבִיא
אֶל־הַתֵּבָה לְהַחֲיֹת אִתָּךְ זָכָר
וּנְקֵבָה יִהְיוּ: מֵהָעוֹף לְמִינֵהוּ
וּמִן־הַבְּהֵמָה לְמִינָהּ מִכֹּל
רֶמֶשׂ הָאֲדָמָה לְמִינֵהוּ שְׁנַיִם
מִכֹּל יָבֹאוּ אֵלֶיךָ לְהַחֲיוֹת:
וְאַתָּה קַח־לְךָ מִכָּל־מַאֲכָל
אֲשֶׁר יֵאָכֵל וְאָסַפְתָּ אֵלֶיךָ
וְהָיָה לְךָ וְלָהֶם לְאָכְלָה: וַיַּעַשׂ
נֹחַ כְּכֹל אֲשֶׁר צִוָּה אֹתוֹ אֱלֹהִים

CRITICAL NOTES.

Noah and the Ark : Section vi, 13-22, is P, and Section vii, 1-5, is J and his redactors. Higher Criticism finds here two authors in the main. Yet it will be seen from the results of Reconstructive Criticism that P is most composite, by no means the work of one hand. This failure of Higher Criticism to distinguish in this place and elsewhere continuous homogeneous narratives accounts for its resort to redactions to account for incongruities. The two narratives, as given by Reconstructive Criticism, are similar in that a divine command is laid upon Noah to build the ark for himself and family, and for such of animal life as were to be preserved, because

GENERATIONS OF NOAH.

6, 7 the face of the ground; both man, and beast, and creeping thing, and fowl of the air; for it repenteth me that I have made them. Noah was a righteous man, perfect in his **8** generations: and Noah found grace in the eyes of Jehovah.

NOAH AND THE ARK.

7, 1 And Jehovah said unto Noah,
6, 14 Make thee an ark of gopher wood. And this is how thou shalt make **15** it: the length of the ark three hundred cubits, the breadth of it fifty cubits, and the height of it thirty **16** cubits. And to a cubit thou shalt finish it upwards. With lower, second, and third stories thou shalt
7, 1 make it. Enter thou and all thy
6, 18 house into the ark, and I will establish my covenant with thee;
7, 1 for thee have I seen righteous be-**2** fore me in this generation. Of every clean beast thou shalt take to thee seven and seven, the male and his female; also of the fowl of the air, male and female. And of the beasts that are not clean, **3** two, the male and his female: to keep seed alive upon the face of **4** all the earth. For yet seven days, and I will cause it to rain upon the earth forty days and forty nights; and every living thing that I have
6, 17 made will I destroy from off the face of the ground. Every thing that
7, 5 is in the earth, shall die. And Noah did according unto all that Jehovah commanded him.

כְּנֵי הָאֲדָמָה מֵאָדָם עַד־בְּהֵמָה עַד־רֶמֶשׂ וְעַד־עוֹף הַשָּׁמָיִם כִּי נִחַמְתִּי כִּי עֲשִׂיתִם: נֹחַ אִישׁ צַדִּיק תָּמִים הָיָה בְּדֹרֹתָיו:וְנֹחַ מָצָא חֵן בְּעֵינֵי יְהוָה:

וַיֹּאמֶר יְהוָה לְנֹחַ עֲשֵׂה לְךָ תֵּבַת עֲצֵי־גֹפֶר:וְזֶה עֲשֶׂר תַּעֲשֶׂה אֹתָהּ שְׁלֹשׁ מֵאוֹת אַמָּה אֹרֶךְ הַתֵּבָה חֲמִשִּׁים אַמָּה רָחְבָּהּ וּשְׁלֹשִׁים אַמָּה קוֹמָתָהּ: וְאֶל־אַמָּה תְּכַלֶּנָּה מִלְמַעְלָה: תַּחְתִּיִּם שְׁנִיִּם וּשְׁלִשִׁים תַּעֲשֶׂהָ: בֹּא־אַתָּה וְכָל־בֵּיתְךָ אֶל־הַתֵּבָה הֲקִמֹתִי אֶת־בְּרִיתִי אִתְּךָ כִּי־ אֹתְךָ רָאִיתִי צַדִּיק לְפָנַי בַּדּוֹר הַזֶּה:מִכֹּל הַבְּהֵמָה הַטְּהוֹרָה תִּקַּח־לְּךָ שִׁבְעָה שִׁבְעָה אִישׁ וְאִשְׁתּוֹ:גַּם מֵעוֹף הַשָּׁמַיִם זָכָר וּנְקֵבָה:וּמִן הַבְּהֵמָה אֲשֶׁר לֹא טְהֹרָה הִוא לְ שְׁנַיִם אִישׁ וְאִשְׁתּוֹ לְחַיּוֹת זֶרַע עַל־פְּנֵי כָל־הָאָרֶץ:כִּי לְיָמִים עוֹד שִׁבְעָה אָנֹכִי מַמְטִיר עַל־הָאָרֶץ אַרְבָּעִים יוֹם וְאַרְבָּעִים לַיְלָה וּמָחִיתִי אֶת־כָּל־הַיְקוּם אֲשֶׁר עָשִׂיתִי מֵעַל פְּנֵי הָאֲדָמָה: כֹּל אֲשֶׁר בָּאָרֶץ יִגְוָע:וַיַּעַשׂ נֹחַ כְּכֹל אֲשֶׁר צִוָּהוּ יְהוָה:

CRITICAL NOTES.

God was about to bring the flood upon the earth. All else varies. The ark in each narrative is different; the animals enter under a different numerical order in each. The priestly writer employs the words "clean and unclean, righteous," words associated with temple worship. The prophetic writer employs in his narrative words which he used in his account of Creation. The details of the Prophetic Narrative are more natural : a window is made in the ark for light, and food is taken in the ark for all the living. The Priestly Narrative omits these facts, but gives us dimensions, and a separate story for man, and the clean animals, and the unclean.

so did he.

כן עשה:

THE FLOOD.

7, 6 And Noah was six hundred years old when the flood of waters was
7 upon the earth. And Noah went in, and his sons and his wife, and his sons' wives with him, into the ark, because of the waters of the
14 flood. They, and every beast after its kind, and all cattle after their kind, and every creeping thing that creepeth upon the earth after its kind, and every fowl after its kind, every bird of every sort.
15 And they went in unto Noah into the ark, two and two of all flesh
16 wherein is the breath of life. And they that went in, went in male and female of all flesh, as God
17 commanded him. And the flood was forty days upon the earth;
18 and the waters increased and bare up the ark, and it was lifted above
19 the earth. And the waters prevailed exceedingly upon the earth; and all the high mountains that were under the whole heavens were
21 covered. And every living thing was destroyed which was upon the face of the ground, both man, and cattle, and creeping thing, and fowl of the heaven; and they were destroyed from the earth: and Noah

וַיְהִי נֹחַ בֶּן־שֵׁשׁ מֵאוֹת שָׁנָה וְהַמַּבּוּל
הָיָה מַיִם עַל־הָאָרֶץ: וַיָּבֹא נֹחַ
וּבָנָיו וְאִשְׁתּוֹ וּנְשֵׁי־בָנָיו אִתּוֹ אֶל־
הַתֵּבָה מִפְּנֵי מֵי הַמַּבּוּל:
הֵמָּה וְכָל־הַחַיָּה לְמִינָהּ וְכָל־
הַבְּהֵמָה לְמִינָהּ וְכָל־הָרֶמֶשׂ
הָרֹמֵשׂ עַל־הָאָרֶץ לְמִינֵהוּ
וְכָל־הָעוֹף לְמִינֵהוּ כֹּל צִפּוֹר
כָּל־כָּנָף: וַיָּבֹאוּ אֶל־נֹחַ אֶל־
הַתֵּבָה שְׁנַיִם שְׁנַיִם מִכָּל־הַבָּשָׂר
אֲשֶׁר־בּוֹ רוּחַ חַיִּים: וְהַבָּאִים זָכָר
וּנְקֵבָה מִכָּל־בָּשָׂר בָּאוּ כַּאֲשֶׁר אֹתוֹ
אֱלֹהִים וַיְהִי הַמַּבּוּל אַרְבָּעִים
יוֹם עַל־הָאָרֶץ וַיִּרְבּוּ הַמַּיִם
וַיִּשְׂאוּ אֶת־הַתֵּבָה וַתָּרָם
מֵעַל הָאָרֶץ: וְהַמַּיִם גָּבְרוּ
מְאֹד מְאֹד עַל־הָאָרֶץ וַיְכֻסּוּ
כָּל־הֶהָרִים הַגְּבֹהִים אֲשֶׁר־
תַּחַת כָּל־הַשָּׁמָיִם: וַיִּמַח אֶת־
כָּל־הַיְקוּם אֲשֶׁר עַל־פְּנֵי
הָאֲדָמָה מֵאָדָם עַד־בְּהֵמָה
עַד־רֶמֶשׂ וְעַד־עוֹף הַשָּׁמַיִם
וַיִּמָּחוּ מִן־הָאָרֶץ וַיִּשָּׁאֶר אַךְ־
נֹחַ וַאֲשֶׁר אִתּוֹ בַּתֵּבָה: וַיִּגְבְּרוּ
הַמַּיִם עַל־הָאָרֶץ חֲמִשִּׁים
וּמְאַת יוֹם:

24 only was left, and they who were with him in the ark. And the waters prevailed upon the earth an hundred and fifty days.

CRITICAL NOTES.

The Flood : Higher Criticism analyzes this portion as follows : V. 6 is P ; vv. 7-10 is J and his redactors : v. 11 is P ; v. 12 is J ; vv. 13-15 is P ; vv. 16-17 is P and J ; vv. 18-21 is P : vv. 2, 3, is J and his redactors ; v. 24 is P. This analysis proves only that there is confusion in the account as we find it in the text. Reconstructive Criticism disentangles this confusion, and finds two accounts, each full, each with its characteristic differences, each nevertheless confirming the other. The Prophetic Narrative and the Priestly Narrative are essentially alike as to facts ; they vary as to details, yet only such kind of variation as we have become

THE FLOOD.

7, 13; In the selfsame day entered Noah, and Shem, and Ham, and Japheth, the sons of Noah, and Noah's wife, and the three wives of his sons with them, into the ark. Of clean beasts, and of beasts that are not clean, and of fowls, and of every thing which creepeth 9 upon the ground, there went in 3 seven and seven, two and two, un- 9 to Noah into the ark, male and female, according as God had com- 16 manded Noah. And Jehovah shut 16 him in. And it came to pass after seven days, that the waters of the 11 flood were upon the earth. In the six hundredth year of Noah's life, in the second month, on the seventeenth day of the month, on the same day were all the fountains of the great deep broken up, and the windows of heaven were open. 12 And there was rain upon the earth 13 forty days and forty nights. And the waters prevailed, and increased greatly upon the earth; and the ark went upon the face of the 20 waters. Fifteen cubits upward did the waters prevail; and the 21 mountains were covered. And all flesh that moved upon the

בעצם היום הזה בא נח ושם
וחם ויפת בני-נח ואשת נח
ושלשת נשי-בניו אתם אל-
התבה: מן-הבהמה הטהורה
ומן-הבהמה אשר איננה
טהרה ומן-העוף וכל אשר
רמש על-האדמה: שנים 4
שנים שבעה שבעה באו אל-
נח אל-התבה זכר ונקבה
כאשר צוה אלהים את-נח:
ויסגר יהוה בעדו ויהי לשבעת
הימים ומי המבול היו על-
הארץ: בשנת שש-מאות שנה
לחיי-נח בחדש השני בשבעה-
עשר יום לחדש ביום הנה
נבקעו כל-מעינות תהון רבה
וארבת השמים נפתחו ויהי
הגשם על-הארץ ארבעים
יום וארבעים לילה: ויגברו
המים וירבו מאד על-הארץ
ותלך התבה על-פני-המים:
חמש עשרה אמה מלמעלה
גברו המים ויכסו ההרים:
ויגוע כל-בשר הרמש על-
הארץ בעוף ובבהמה ובחיה
ובכל-השרץ השרץ על-הארץ
וכל-האדם: כל אשר נשמת-
רוח חיים באפו מכל-אשר

earth died, both fowl, and cattle, and beast, and every creep- 22 ing thing that creepeth upon the earth, and every man. Everything in whose nostrils was the breath of life, of all that

CRITICAL NOTES.

familiar with. Most careful time-designations are recorded in the Priestly Narrative. The prophetic writer gives here the duration of the continuance of the waters in this portion; the priestly will give this fact in the succeeding portion. An elaborate argument to prove the unity of these two narratives may be drawn from linguistic considerations; but this aid can not be invoked in notes, such as we confine ourself to. Yet there is in the two narratives of Reconstructive Criticism a convincing argument of truth in their consistent parts, and in the evident independence of each, combined with a different point of view which each writer maintains.

ABATEMENT OF THE WATERS.

8, 1 And God remembered Noah, and every living thing, and all the cattle that were with him in the ark: and God made a wind to pass over the earth, and the waters assuaged.
5 And the waters returned from off
6 the earth continually. And it came to pass at the end of forty days, that Noah opened the window of
7 the ark, which he had made: and sent forth a raven, and it went forth to and fro, until the waters were dried up from off the earth.
8 And he sent forth a dove from him, to see if the waters were abated from off the face of the
9 ground; but the dove found no rest for the sole of her foot, and she returned unto him to the ark, for the waters were on the face of the whole earth: and he put forth his hand, and took her, and brought her in unto him into
10 the ark. And he stayed yet other seven days; and again he sent forth the dove out of the ark; and the dove came in to him at even-
11 tide; and, lo, in her mouth an olive leaf pluckt off: so Noah knew that the waters were abated from off the
12 face of the earth. And he stayed yet other seven days; and sent forth the dove; and she returned not
13 again unto him any more. And Noah removed the covering of the ark, and looked out, and, behold, the face of the ground was dry.

ויזכר אלהים את־נח ואת כל־
החיה ואת־כל־הבהמה אשר
אתו בתבה ויעבר אלהים רוח
על־הארץ וישכו המים:וישבו
המים מעל הארץ הלוך
ושוב:ויהי מקץ ארבעים יום
ויפתח נח את־הלון התבה
אשר עשה:וישלח את־הערב
ויצא יצוא ושוב עד־יבשת
המים מעל הארץ:וישלח
את־היונה מאתו לראות הקלו
המים מעל פני האדמה:ולא־
מצאה היונה מנוח לכף־רגלה
ותשב אליו אל־התבה כי־
מים על־פני כל־ה ארץ
וישלח ידו ויקחה ויבא אתה
אליו אל־התבה:ויחל עוד
שבעת ימים אחרים ויסף
שלח את־היונה מן־התבה
ותבא אליו היונה לעת־ערב
והנה עלה־זית טרף בפיה:
וידע נח כי־קלו המים מעל
הארץ:וייחל עוד שבעת ימים
אחרים וישלח את־היונה ולא־
יספה שוב־אליו עוד:ויסר נח
את־מכסה התבה וירא והנה
חרבו פני האדמה:

CRITICAL NOTES.

Abatement of the Waters: The documents of this section, according to Higher Criticism, are: vv. viii, 1-2, is P; v. 3 is J; vv. 4-5 is P; vv. 6-12 is J; v. 13 is P and J; v. 14 is P. It is to be observed that much which Higher Criticism relegates to one document is a duplicate portion under the view of Reconstructive Criticism. A remarkable characteristic of the Prophetic Narrative is seen in this section. The prophetic writer recognizes the ordinary prudential measures which man takes. Noah finds out by experiment whether the waters are abated from off the face of the earth. He sends forth a raven first, then a dove. This same writer observes,

7, 23 was in the dry land, died.

ABATEMENT OF THE
WATERS.

8, 2   And the fountains of the deep
and the windows of heaven were
stopped, and the rain from heaven
3 was restrained; and the waters decreased after an hundred and fifty
4 days. And the ark rested in the
seventh month, on the seventeenth
day of the month, upon the moun-
5 tain of Ararat. And the waters
decreased continually until the
tenth month : in the tenth month,
on the first day of the month, were
the tops of the mountains seen.
13 And it came to pass in the six
hundredth and first year, in the
first month, in the first day of the
month, the waters were dried from
14 off the earth. And in the second
month, and the twentieth day of
the mouth, the earth was dry.

נחרבה סתו:

ויסכרו מעינת תהום וארבת
השמים ויכלא הגשם מן—
השמים:ויחסרו המים מקצה
חמשים ומאַ ת יום:ותנח
התבה · בחרש השביעי בשנה-
עשר יום לחרש על הרי
ארר֯ט:והמים היו הלוך וחסור
עד־ ה חרש הַעשירי בעשורי
באחד לחתש נראו רשי ההרם
ויהי באחת ישושו-מאות שנה
בראשון באחד לחרש חרבה
המים מעל הארץ:ובחרש
השני בשבעה ועשרים יום
לחרש יבשה הארץ.

CRITICAL NOTES.

that the waters were assuaged, because God made a wind to pass over the earth.
The priestly writer in this part confines himself strictly to an exact chronology.
There is no contradiction in the two narratives. They are alike in the fact
recorded. They are diverse in the incidents. The prophetic writer loves to behold
man co-operating with God in the emergencies, while the priestly is most bent
upon seeing what God does for man apart from this co-operation. Hence the incident of the sending forth of the raven and the dove is a prophetic record.

DEPARTURE FROM THE ARK.

8, 18 And Noah went forth, and his sons, and his wife, and his sons'
19 wives with him: every beast, every creeping thing, and every fowl, whatsoever moveth upon the earth, after their families, went forth out
9, 1 of the ark. And God blessed Noah and his sons, and said to them, Be fruitful, and multiply, and fill the
2 earth. And the fear of you be upon every beast of the earth, and
3 upon every fowl of the air. Every moving thing that liveth shall be to you, as the green herb, for food.
4 Into your hand are they given. I
5 will require the life of man from the hand of every man's brother.
6 Whosoever sheddeth man's blood, by man shall his blood be shed; for in the image of God made he
12 man. And God said, And I, be-
9 hold, I establish my covenant be-
12 tween me and you, and every living creature that is with you, for
8, 22 perpetual generations: while the earth remaineth, seedtime and harvest, and cold and heat, and summer and winter, and day and night shall not cease. And there shall not be any more a flood to destroy
9, 13 the earth. I set my bow in the cloud, and it shall be for a token of a covenant between me and the
16 earth. And the bow shall be in the cloud; and I will look upon it, that I may remember the everlasting covenant between God and every living creature of all flesh that is upon the earth.

ויצא נח ובניו ואשתו ונשי בניו
אתו:כל־החיה כל־הרמש וכל־
העוף כל־רומש על־הארץ
למשפחתיהם יצאו מן־התבה:
ויברך אלהים את־נח ואת־בניו ויאמר
להם פרו ורבו וסלאו את־
הארץ:ומוראכם יהיה על כל־
חית הארץ ועל כל־עוף השמים
כל רמש אשר הוא חי לכם יהיה
לכם כירק עשב לא אכלה:
בידכם נתנו:ומיד איש אחיו
אדרש את־נפש האדם:שפך דם
האדם באדם דמו ישפך לצלם
האדם עשה את־יה ארם:ויאמר
אלהים ואני הנני מקים כב
בריתי ביני וביניכם ובין כל
חיה אשר אתכם לדרת
עולם:עד כל־ימי הארץ זרע
וקציר קר וחם וקיץ וחרף
ויום ולילה לא ישבתו:יג
יהיה עוד מבול לשחת הארץ:
את־הקשתי נתתי בענן והיתה
לאות ברית ביני ובין הארץ:
והיתה הקשת בענן וראיתיה
לזכר ברית עולם בין אלהים
ובין כל־נפש חיה בכל־
בשר אשר על־הארץ:

CRITICAL NOTES.

Departure from the Ark: The analysis of Higher Criticism for this passage is quite simple: vv. 15-19 is P; vv. 20-22 is J; vv. ix, 1-17, is P. The utter failure of Higher Criticism to distinguish the narratives in the documents of Genesis comes conspicuously forward in this section. The narratives of Reconstructive Criticism will make this apparent. Each narrative has these facts in common: the departure from the ark, the injunction to increase and multiply, the dominion of man over the animal creation, the reference to murder, the promise of God that the flood should not come again to destroy all flesh, and the bow in the cloud as sign of this prom-

DEPARTURE FROM THE ARK.

8, *15* And God spake unto Noah, say-
16 ing, Go forth from the ark, thou
and thy wife, and thy sons, and
17 thy sons' wives with thee. Bring
forth with thee every living thing
that is with thee of all flesh, both
fowl, and cattle, and every creeping thing that creepeth upon the
earth; that they may breed abundantly in the earth, and be fruitful
19 and multiply upon the earth. And
20 they went forth from the ark. And
Noah built an altar unto Jehovah;
and took of every clean beast, and
of every clean fowl, and offered
burnt offerings upon the altar.
21 And Jehovah smelled the sweet
savor; and Jehovah said in his
heart, I will not again curse any
more the ground for man's sake,
for the imagination of man's heart
is evil from his youth; neither
will I again smite any more every
9, *8* living thing, as I have done. And
God spake to Noah, and to his
7 sons with him, saying, And you,
be ye fruitful and multiply; bring
forth abundantly in the earth, and
2 multiply therein. And the dread
of you be with all wherewith the
ground teemeth, and with all the
3 fishes of the sea. I give to you
10 all belonging to all the life of the
4 earth. Only the flesh itself, not its

וירבר אלהים אל־נח לאמר:
צא מן־התבה אתה ואשתך
ובניך ונשי־בניך אתך:כל־החיה
אשר אתך הוצא מכל־
בשר בעוף ובבהמה ובכל־הרמש
הרמש של־ה־ארץ:וישרצ
בארץ ופרו ורבו עֵל־ה־ארץ:
ויצאו מן־התבה:ויבן נח
מזבח ליהוה ויקח מכל
הבהמה השהרה ומכל
השוף השהור ויעל
עלֹת במזבח: וירח
יהוה את־ריח הניחה
ויאטר יהוה אל־לבו
לא אסף להלל עוד
את־ה־ארמה בעבור הארס
כי יצר לב האדם רע
מנעריו ולא אסף עוד להכת
את־כל־חי כאשר עשתי
ויאמר אלהַ אל־נח ואל־בניו
אתו לאמר:ואחס פרו ורבו
שרצו בארץ ורבו־בה:וחתלם
בכל אשר תרמש הארמה,
ובכל רגי הים:נתתי לכם
את־כל לכול חית הארֹץ: אף
בשר בנפשו רמו לא תאכלו:
ואך את רםכם לנפשתיכם
ארדרש· מיד כל־חיה ארדשנו
ומיד הארם:ויאמר אלהים אל־
נח והקמתי את־בריתי אתְ־כם
ואת־ידעכם אחריכם:ואת־כל

5 blood, shalt thou eat. And surely your blood among you yourselves I
shall seek: from the hand of every beast I will seek it, and from the
11 17 hand of man. And God said to Noah, And I will establish my
9 covenant with you and with your seed after you, and with every

CRITICAL NOTES.

ise. Yet there are decided variations. The priestly writer says that Noah went
forth from the ark by command of Jehovah; that Noah offered an offering unto Jehovah upon an altar; that flesh is given to man for food, but blood must not be
eaten: that Jehovah will surely require the life of man from all who destroy it, man
or beast. The prophetic writer says that Noah went out of the ark; that God
blessed him: that meat and the herb was given to man for food; that God established here the law against murder. There was need for the priestly writer only to
repeat the sacredness of human life, because the narrative concerning Cain and

NOAH'S CURSE UPON
CANAAN.

9, 19 Shem, Ham, and Japheth, these
were the sons of Noah: and of
these was the whole earth over-
20 spread. And Noah began to be a
husbandman, and planted a vine-
21 yard; and he drank of the wine,
and was drunken; and he was un-
22 covered within his tent. And Ham,
the father of Canaan, saw the
nakedness of his father, and told
23 his two brethren without. And
Shem and Japheth took a garment,
and covered the nakedness of their
father; and their faces were backward, and the nakedness of their
24 father they saw not. And Noah
awoke from his wine, and knew
what his youngest son had done
25 unto him. And he said,
 Cursed be Canaan;
 A servant of servants
 Let him be unto his brethren.
28 And Noah lived after the flood three

שֵׁם וְחָם וָיָפֶת אֵלֶּה בְּנֵי־נֹחַ
וּמֵאֵלֶּה נָפְצָה כָל־הָאָרֶץ: וַיָּחֶל
נֹחַ אִישׁ הָאֲדָמָה וַיִּשַּׁע כָּרֶם: וַיֵּשְׁתְּ
מִן־הַיַּיִן וַיִּשְׁכָּר וַיִּתְגַּל בְּתוֹךְ
אָהֳלֹה: וַיַּרְא חָם אֲבִי כְנַעַן
אֵת עֶרְוַת אָבִיו וַיַּגֵּד לִשְׁנֵי־
אֶחָיו בַּחוּץ: וַיִּקַּח שֵׁם וָיָפֶת אֶת
הַשִּׂמְלָה וַיָּשִׂימוּ אֵת עֶרְוַת עָלֵיהֶם
וּפְנֵיהֶם אֲחֹרַנִּית וְעֶרְוַת צְבִיהֶם
לֹא רָאוּ: וַיִּיקֶץ נֹחַ מִיֵּינוֹ וַיֵּדַע
אֵת אֲשֶׁר־עָשָׂה לוֹ בְּנוֹ הַקָּטָן:
וַיֹּאמֶר

אָרוּר כְּנָעַן
עֶבֶד עֲבָדִים
יִהְיֶה לְאֶחָיו:
וַיְחִי־נֹחַ אַחַר הַמַּבּוּל שְׁלֹשׁ

CRITICAL NOTES.

Abel had declared the law. The prophetic writer declared the law for the first
time. He also refers to his Creation narrative in the words "as the green herb."
It is the prophetic writer that knows of the everlasting covenant which God makes
with man. The great flood interpolation of Higher Criticism falls to the ground in
the face of these two narratives of Reconstructive Criticism.

Noah's Curse upon Canaan: The portion ix, 18-27, is assigned to J and his redactors; vv. 28-29 is recognized as P, under the view of Higher Criticism. Yet there
are two distinct accounts here. The peculiarity of the priestly writer appears mostly
in the words announcing the curse. He declares Jehovah to be the God of Shem.
He records that Noah implores God to give Japheth a dwelling-place in the tents of

DEPARTURE FROM THE ARK.

9, 10 living creature that is with you,
the fowl, the cattle, and every beast
of the earth with you ; of all that
11 go out of the ark.   And not shall
all flesh be cut off any more by
12 the waters of the flood. This is
the sign of the covenant which I
14 make : and it shall come to pass
15 when I bring a cloud over the
earth, that the bow shall be seen
in the cloud, and I will remember
my covenant, which is between me
and you and every living creature
of all flesh ; and the waters shall
not become any more a flood to
17 destroy all flesh. This is the sign
of the covenant which I establish
between me and all flesh that is
upon the earth.

נֶפֶשׁ הַחַיָּה אֲשֶׁר אִתְּכֶם בָּעוֹף
בַּבְּהֵמָה וּבְכָל־חַיַּת הָאָרֶץ אִתְּכֶם
מִכֹּל יֹצְאֵי הַתֵּבָה׃וְלֹא־יִכָּרֵת
כָּל־בָּשָׂר עוֹד מִמֵּי הַמַּבּוּל׃
זֹאת אוֹת־הַבְּרִית אֲשֶׁר־אֲנִי נֹתֵן
וְהָיְתָה בֶּעָנָן עֲלֵיהָ הָאָרֶץ׃
וְנִרְאֲתָה הַקֶּשֶׁת בֶּעָנָן׃
וְזָכַרְתִּי אֶת־בְּרִיתִי אֲשֶׁר בֵּינִי
וּבֵינֵיכֶם וּבֵין כָּל־נֶפֶשׁ חַיָּה
בְּכָל־בָּשָׂר וְלֹא־יִהְיֶה עוֹד
הַמַּיִם לְמַבּוּל לְשַׁחֵת כָּל־
בָּשָׂר׃ זֹאת אוֹת הַבְּרִית אֲשֶׁר
הֲקִמֹתִי בֵּנִי וּבֵין כָּל־בָּשָׂר אֲשֶׁר
הָאָרֶץ׃

NOAH'S CURSE UPON CANAAN.

9, 18 The sons of Noah, that went
forth of the ark, were three, Shem,
Ham, and Japheth ; and Ham was
20 the father of Canaan. And Noah
began to be an husbandman, and
21 planted a vineyard ; and he drank
of the wine, and was drunken ; and
22 was uncovered in his tent. And
Ham saw the nakedness of his
father, and told his two brethren
23 without. And Shem and Japheth
took a garment, and laid it upon

וַיִּהְיוּ שְׁלֹשָׁה בְּנֵי־נֹחַ הַיֹּצְאִים
מִן־הַתֵּבָה שֵׁם וְחָם וָיָפֶת
וְחָם הוּא אֲבִי־כְנָעַן׃וְיָחֶל
נֹחַ אִישׁ הָאֲדָמָה׃וַיִּטַּע כָּרֶם׃
וַיֵּשְׁתְּ מִן־הַיַּיִן וַיִּשְׁכָּר וַיִּתְגַּל
בְּתוֹךְ אָהֳלֹה׃וַיַּרְא חָם אֶת
עֶרְוַת אָבִיו וַיַּגֵּד לִשְׁנֵי־אֶחָיו
בַּחוּץ׃וַיִּקַּח שֵׁם וָיֶפֶת אֶת־
הַשִּׂמְלָה וַיָּשִׂימוּ עַל־שְׁכֶם
שְׁנֵיהֶם וַיֵּלְכוּ אֲחֹרַנִּית וַיְכַסּוּ
אֵת־עֶרְוַת אֲבִיהֶם׃וַיִּיקֶץ נֹחַ
מִיֵּינוֹ וַיֵּדַע אֵת אֲשֶׁר־עָשָׂה
לוֹ בְּנוֹ הַקָּטָן׃וַיֹּאמֶר
בָּרוּךְ יְהֹוָה אֱלֹהֵי שֵׁם
וִיהִי כְנַעַן עֶבֶד לָמוֹ׃
יַפְתְּ אֱלֹהִים לְיֶפֶת

both of their shoulders, and went backward, and covered the nakedness
24 of their father. And Noah awoke from his wine, and knew what his
26 youngest son had done unto him. And he said,
Blessed be Jehovah, the God of Shem ;
And let Canaan be his servant.
God enlarge Japheth,

CRITICAL NOTES.

Shem. This same writer in the narrative portion is more circumstantial ; for he
tells of Shem and Japheth laying the garment upon their shoulders. The prophetic writer records the same facts, yet he is briefer. There is prophetic energy in
the conciseness of the words of the curse. It is to be observed, also, that the prophetic writer has no mention of God in the curse upon Ham.

NOAH'S CURSE UPON CANAAN.

hundred and fifty years. מאת שנה וחמשים שנה:

NOAH'S CURSE UPON CANAAN.

9, 27 And let him dwell in the tents of Shem;
And let Canaan be his servant.
29 And all the days of Noah were nine hundred and fifty years: and he died.

וישכן באהלי־ שם
ויהי כנען עבד למו:
ויהי כל־ימי־ נח תשע מאות
שנה וחמשים שנה וימת:

THE DISPERSION.

11, 1 And the whole earth was one language and one speech. And it came
2 to pass, as they journeyed east, that they found a plain in the land of
3 Shinar; and they dwelt there. And they said one to another, Go to, let us make brick, and burn them thoroughly. And they had brick for stone, and slime had they for mor-
4 tar. And they said, Go to, let us build us a city, and a tower, whose top shall be in the heavens, and let us make us a name; lest we be scattered abroad upon the face of
6 the whole earth. And Jehovah
7 said, Go to, let us go down to see
5 the city and the tower, which the
6 children of men are building. Then this is the beginning of what they do, and now nothing will be withholden from them, which they purpose to do. Behold, they are one people, and they have all one lan-
7 guage; now let us confound there their language, that they may not understand one another's speech.
8 And Jehovah came down, that there Jehovah might confound
9 the language of all the earth, and that thence Jehovah might scatter them abroad upon the face of all the earth. Therefore
8 was the name of it called Babel. So Jehovah scattered them

CRITICAL NOTES.

The Dispersion: Higher Criticism finds xi, 1–9, to be the work of J. The inconsistencies of the account are passed over. Reconstructive Criticism traces a consistent narrative, and assigns it to the priestly writer. The form of the narrative, as men speak among themselves, is like that which Jehovah employs when he talks here to himself. A comparison with the reconstructed text will show how much distorted is the received text. The love of the priestly writer for those old traditions, which enshrine some truths of the earliest times, is again evinced here. The name Babel, with him, is the human testimony to the deed of Jehovah, when he scattered men abroad over the earth.

3

GENERATIONS OF THE SONS OF NOAH.

10, 32 These are the families of the sons of Noah according to their generations among their nations: And of these were the nations overspread in the earth after the 1 flood. Shem, and Ham, and Japheth; and sons were born to them after the flood. The sons of Japheth; Gomer, and Magog, and Madai, and Javan, and Tubal, and Meshech, and Tiras. And the sons of Gomer; Ashkenaz, and Riphath, and Togarmah. And the sons of Javan; Elishah, and Tarshish, Kittim, and Dodanim. Of these were the isles of the nations overspread after their families, among the nations. And the sons of Ham; Cush, and Mizraim, and Put, and Canaan. And the sons of Cush; Seba, and Havilah, and Sabtah, and Raamah, and Sabteca. And the sons of Raamah; Sheba, and Dedan. And Cush begat Nimrod: and he began to be great in the earth. And Mizraim begat Ludim, and Anamim, and Lehabim, and Naphtuhim, and Pathrusim, and Casluhim, (whence went forth the Philistines) and the Caphtorim. And Canaan begat Zidon, his first-born, and Heth, and the Jebusite, and the Amorite, and the Girgashite; and the Hivite, and the Arkite, and the Sinite; and the Arvadite, and the Zemarite, and the Hamathite: and afterwards the families of the Canaanites spread abroad, as thou goest

אֵלֶּה מִשְׁפְּחֹת בְּנֵי־נֹחַ לְתֹלְדֹתָם
בְּגוֹיֵהֶם וּמֵאֵלֶּה נִפְרְדוּ הַגּוֹיִם
בָּאָרֶץ אַחַר הַמַּבּוּל: שֵׁם וְהֶם
יֶפֶת וַיִּוָּלְדוּ לָהֶם בָּנִים אַחַר
הַמַּבּוּל: בְּנֵי יֶפֶת גֹּמֶר וּמָגוֹג
וּמָדַי וְיָוָן וְתֻבָל וּמֶשֶׁךְ וְתִירָס:
וּבְנֵי גֹּמֶר אַשְׁכְּנַז וְרִיפַת
וְתֹגַרְמָה: וּבְנֵי יָוָן אֱלִישָׁה
וְתַרְשִׁישׁ כִּתִּים וְדֹדָנִים:
מֵאֵלֶּה נִפְרְדוּ אִיֵּי־הַגּוֹיִם
בְּמַפְצֹחְתָם בְּגוֹיֵם רַבְנֵי חָם
כּוּשׁ וּמִצְרַיִם וּפוּט וּכְנַעַן:
וּבְנֵי כוּשׁ סְבָא וַחֲוִילָה וְסַבְתָּה
וְרַעְמָה וְסַבְתְּכָא וּבְנֵי רַעְמָה
שְׁבָא וּדְדָן וְכוּשׁ יָלַד אֶת־
נִמְרֹד הוּא הֵחֵל לִהְיוֹת גִּבֹּר
בָּאָרֶץ וּמִצְרַיִם יָלַד אֶת־לוּדִים
אֶת־עֲנָמִים וְאֶת־לְהָבִים וְאֶת־
נַפְתֻּחִים וְאֶת־פַּתְרֻסִים וְאֶת־
כַּסְלֻחִים אֲשֶׁר יָצְאוּ מִשָּׁם פְּלִשְׁתִּים
וְאֶת־כַּפְתֹּרִם וּכְנַעַן יָלַד אֶת־
צִידֹן בְּכֹרוֹ וְאֶת־חֵת: וְאֶת־
הַיְבוּסִי וְאֶת־הָאֱמֹרִי וְאֶת־
הַגִּרְגָּשִׁי וְאֶת־הַחִוִּי וְאֶת־הָעַרְקִי
וְאֶת־הַסִּינִי: וְאֶת־הָאַרְוָדִי וְאֶת־
הַצְּמָרִי וְאֶת־הַחֲמָתִי וְאַחַר
נָפֹצוּ מִשְׁפְּחוֹת הַכְּנַעֲנִי בָּאֵלֶּה

CRITICAL NOTES.

Generations of the Sons of Noah: The tenth chapter of Genesis is most remarkable for its tables of genealogies. It is most composite according to Higher Criticism. This portion is assigned to documents as follows: x, 1, is P and J; vv. 2-7 is P; vv. 8-19 is J and his redactors; v. 20 is P; v. 21 is J; vv. 22-23 is P; vv. 24-30 is J; vv. 31-32 is P. The table is a kind of patch-work. A most remarkable confirmation of the theory of Reconstructive Criticism comes to the front in its treatment of this table. It was found that in the two accounts of Noah's curse upon Canaan there was some common matter. Yet only such matter as must of necessity be

THE DISPERSION.

thence upon the face of all the
11, ⁵ earth; and they left off to build
the city.

משם עליפני כל־האר ץ
ויחדלו לבנת העיר׃

GENERATIONS OF THE SONS OF NOAH.

10, 1 And these are the generations of
the sons of Noah, Shem, Ham and
2 Japheth. The sons of Japheth;
Gomer, and Magog, and Madai, and
Javan, and Tubal, and Meshech,
3 and Tiras. And the sons of Gomer; Ashkenaz, and Riphath, and
4 Togarmah. And the sons of Javan; Elishah, and Tarshish, Kit-
5 tim, and Dodanim. Of these were
the isles of the nations divided into
their lands, every one after his
6 tongue. And the sons of Ham;
Cush, and Mizraim, and Put, and
7 Canaan. And the sons of Cush,
Seba, and Havilah, and Sabtah,
and Raamah, and Sabteca. And
the sons of Raamah, Sheba, and
8 Dedan. And Cush begat Nimrod:
and he began to be a mighty one in
9 the earth. He was a mighty hunter
before Jehovah: wherefore it is
said, Like Nimrod a mighty hunter
10 before Jehovah. And the beginning
of his kingdom was Babel, and
Erech, and Accad, and Calneh, in the
11 land of Shinar. Out of that land he
went forth into Assyria, and builded
12 Nineveh, and Rehoboth-Ir, and Calah, and Resen between Nineveh and
13 Calah; the same is the great city. And Mizraim begat Ludim, and
14 Anamim, and Lehabim, and Naphtuhim, and the Pathrusim, and the

ואלה תולדת בני־נח שם
חם ויפת: ובני יפת גמר
ומגוג ומדי ויון ותבל
ומשך ותירס: ובני גמר
אשכנז וריפת ותגרמה:
ובני יון אלישה ותרשישׁ
כתים ודדנים: מאלה נפרדו
איי הגוים בארצתם ביים
לשנו: ובני חם כוש ומצרים
ופוט וכנען: ובני כוש סבא
וחוילה וסבתה ורעמה
וסבתכא ובני רעמה שבא
ודדן: וכוש ילד את־נמרד
היא החל להיות גבר
בארץ: הוא היה גבר־ציר
לפני יהוה: על־כן יאמר
כנמרד גבור ציר לפני
יהוה: ותהי ראשית ממלכתו
בבל וארך ואכד וכלנה
בארץ שנער: מן־הארץ ההוא
יצא אשור ויבן את־נינוה
ואת־רחבת עיר ואת־כלח:
ואת־רסן בין נינוה ובין
כלח הוא העיר הגדלה: ואת
ומצרים ילד את־לודים ואת־
ענמים ואת־להבים ואת־
נפתחים: ואת־פתרסים ואת

CRITICAL NOTES.

common to a tradition which was inwrought in the very fiber of Hebrew life. Certain liberties were taken in regard to common matter, which is to be found in the
two narratives of the prophetic and priestly writers, by those who wrought them
into the present form. It may be said that certain rules governed those who made
the compositing. These rules are a subject of attractive study. But if there had
been two tables, one common to each of these two narratives, it would have been
impossible to unite them into any kind of discourse without most apparent absurd-
ities. Hence, if such tables existed, a new method must be followed. And it is
found that such a new method was adopted. The table in the prophetic account

www.ingramcontent.com/pod-product-compliance
Lightning Source LLC
Chambersburg PA
CBHW021637270326
41931CB00008B/1058